GUIDE TO BIBLICAL CHRONOLOGY

GUIDE TO BIBLICAL CHRONOLOGY

Antti Laato

SHEFFIELD PHOENIX PRESS

2015

Copyright © 2015 Sheffield Phoenix Press

Published by Sheffield Phoenix Press
Department of Biblical Studies, University of Sheffield
45 Victoria Street
Sheffield S3 7QB

www.sheffieldphoenix.com

All rights reserved.
No part of this publication may be reproduced or transmitted in any form or by any means, electronic or mechanical, including photocopying, recording or any information storage or retrieval system, without the publishers' permission in writing.

A CIP catalogue record for this book
is available from the British Library

Typeset by Forthcoming Publications
Printed by Lightning Source

ISBN 978-1-909697-84-3

CONTENTS

Abbreviations ix

1
INTRODUCTION 1
Why This Book? 1
The Methodological Procedure 2
The Content of This Book 3
Chronology for the Kings of Israel and Judah 4
Albright's Chronology 5
Thiele's Chronology 7
Begrich's and Jepsen's Chronology 8
Hayes's and Hooker's Chronology 10
Hughes's Chronology 11
Galil's Chronology 12
Four Preliminary Questions 13
The New Year 14
Accession-year or Non-accession-year System 17
Co-regency as an Explanation Model 19
Text-critical Considerations Combined with other Speculations 22

2
THE CHRONOLOGICAL DATA OF THE ISRAELITE
AND JUDEAN KINGS 25
Synchronisms and Royal Archives 25
The Biblical Synchronisms of the Israelite and Judean Kings 26
*The Challenge of Extra-biblical Documents
to the Biblical Chronological System* 30

3
RELIABILITY OF THE SYNCHRONIC TRADITION OF THE ISRAELITE AND JUDEAN KINGS — 34
Do We Have a Reliable Tradition for the Biblical Chronology on the Reigns of Kings? — 34
The Case of Uzziah 1 = Jeroboam II 27 — 35
The Case of Omri's Dynasty — 38
The Case of Pekah — 43
Summary — 48

4
THE CHRONOLOGY OF THE LAST JUDEAN KINGS — 50
The Evidence of the Babylonian Chronicle — 50
The Double Dating in Ezekiel 1.1-3 and the Last Kings of Judah — 53

5
THE ABSOLUTE BIBLICAL CHRONOLOGY OF THE BOOKS OF KINGS — 62
Constructed Chronology and its Historical Relevance — 63
    The Invasion of Shishak — 64
    The Battle of Qarqar — 64
    The Tribute of Jehu — 65
    The Tribute of Jehoash — 66
    The Possible Tribute of Azariah/Uzziah — 66
    The Tribute of Menahem — 67
    The Contact of Ahaz to Tiglat-Pileser III — 67
    The Dethronement of Pekah and the Accession of Hosea — 67
    The Destruction of Samaria — 68
    The Invasion of Sennacherib — 68
    The Force Labor Tribute of Manasseh to Esarhaddon — 68
    The Death of Josiah — 68
    The Battle of Carchemish — 69
    The First Conquest of Jerusalem — 69
    The Destruction of Jerusalem — 69
Conclusions: Literacy in Israel — 70
    Seals in Archaeological Excavations — 72
    Monumental Inscriptions — 73
    Early Literary Texts — 73
    Biblical Sources — 73
    Abecedaries — 74

6
THE POSTBIBLICAL CHRONOLOGY AND THE SEVENTY YEARWEEKS IN THE BOOK OF DANIEL — 76
Inaccurate Chronology in the Second Temple Period — 77
The Chronology of Josephus — 79
The Chronology of Demetrius — 82
The Chronology in the Damascus Document — 83
The Chronology in Second Baruch — 86
The Outcome of the Chronological System in Daniel 9.24-27 — 89

7
THE DEUTERONOMISTIC CHRONOLOGICAL FRAMEWORK FOR EARLY ISRAEL — 98

8
THE PRIESTLY CHRONOLOGICAL FRAMEWORK FROM ANNO MUNDI TO PATRIARCHS — 106

9
CONCLUSIONS — 112

Bibliography — 115
Index of References — 123
Index of Authors — 126

ABBREVIATIONS

AB	Anchor Bible
ABD	David Noel Freedman (ed.), *The Anchor Bible Dictionary* (6 vols.; New York: Doubleday, 1992)
ATD	Das Alte Testament Deutsch
BASOR	Bulletin of the American Schools of Oriental Research
BZAW	Beihefte zur Zeitschrift für die alttestamentliche Wissenschaft
CBQ	*Catholic Biblical Quarterly*
ConBOT	Coniectanea biblica, Old Testament
EdF	Erträge der Forschung
EI	*Eretz Israel*
FAT	Forschungen zum Alten Testament
HAT	Handbuch zum Alten Testament
HTR	*Harvard Theological Review*
HUCA	*Hebrew Union College Annual*
ICC	International Critical Commentary
IEJ	*Israel Exploration Journal*
JBL	*Journal of Biblical Literature*
JNES	*Journal of Near Eastern Studies*
JSJSup	Journal for the Study of the Pseudepigrapha, Supplement Series
JSOT	*Journal for the Study of the Old Testament*
JSOTSup	Journal for the Study of the Old Testament, Supplement Series
JSP	*Journal for the Study of the Pseudepigrapha*
JSPSup	Journal for the Study of the Pseudepigrapha, Supplement Series
JSS	*Journal of Semitic Studies*
JTI	*Journal of Theological Interpretation*
KAT	Kommentar zum Alten Testament
KH-CAT	Kurzer Hand-Commentar zum Alten Testament
LCL	Loeb Classical Library
NCB	New Century Bible
OBO	Orbis biblicus et orientalis
OTL	Old Testament Library
OTP	*The Old Testament Pseudepigrapha* (ed. J.H. Charlesworth; 2 vols.; Garden City: Doubleday, 1983–85)
RdQ	*Review de Qumran*
RIMA	The Royal Inscriptions of Mesopotamia, Assyrian Periods
SAAS	State Archives of Assyria Studies
SAOC	Studies in Ancient Oriental Civilizations

SJOT	*Scandinavian Journal of the Old Testament*
TA	*Tel Aviv*
TB	Theologische Bücherei: Neudrucke und Berichte aus dem 20. Jahrhundert
UF	*Ugarit-Forschungen*
VT	*Vetus Testamentum*
VTSup	Vetus Testamentum, Supplement Series
WMANT	Wissenschaftliche Monographien zum Alten und Neuen Testament
WTJ	*Westminster Theological Journal*
ZAW	*Zeitschrift für die Alttestamentliche Wissenschaft*

1

INTRODUCTION

Why This Book?

Every scholar or student working on historical problems understands how essential chronological framework is in every attempt to interpret ancient documents. Often scholars or students are satisfied to apply a given chronology without realizing that there may have been difficult problems which experts had had to solve before providing a nice and fluent chronological framework.

This book is aimed for everyone who wishes to understand why the different chronological proposals exist for the kings of Israel and Judah. The focus is laid on the way of argumentation. The most important question is not to put the biblical chronology in harmony with extrabiblical documents, but rather to demonstrate how the conflicting chronological data preserved in the books of Kings has come about. Only after we have presented a relevant interpretive model for the outcome of the biblical synchronisms can we take another step and connect the model to chronological data of the extrabiblical documents.

The impulse to write this book is my plan to deal with exegetical questions related to Early Israel. Therefore, the elementary basis for this book is not merely a possible hypothetical proposal for the chronology of Israel but rather the fundamental question if we have a reliable chronological skeleton in the form of synchronisms in biblical sources. This means that we are seeking an answer to the question of whether we can regard the synchronisms of the Israelite and Judean kings in the books of Kings as originating from ancient royal archives. Even though we have reason to believe that synchronisms in the books of Kings contain errors, my fundamental methodological question is whether these errors are of such nature that we can explain their outcome in the transmission process. If that is the case this means that we can argue that these synchronisms originate from royal archives and they give us a solid basis for historically reliable chronological framework. If we find that the biblical chronology is based on archival sources this has implications on the literacy in ancient Israel, and that even other textual material in biblical texts (from the exilic and postexilic period) is based on older literal sources.

This being the case, this book does not simply provide a new and plausible chronology for the kings of Israel and Judah, but rather demonstrates how we should argue when we reconstruct such chronology.

In order to make this book more useful for biblical scholars and students I have also added chapters where I deal with postexilic and premonarchic chronologies. I hope that the book can be instructive for everyone who wants to know more about chronological systems which scholars had to reconstruct in order to speak and write about the history of Israel.

The Methodological Procedure

The task of this guide book is to present in which respect chronological traditions in the biblical and ancient Jewish writings can be used as basis for the history of ancient Israel and for the history of the Jewish people in the Second Temple period. We shall seek answers in three different steps. *First*, we shall deal with the biblical and Jewish traditions on their own merits. These traditions may be based on historically reliable chronological records such as, for example, royal annals; or they may be an ancient interpreter's way of structuring historical epochs by using a mathematical-chronological model such as, for example, the seventy yearweeks in Dan. 9.24-27. In this first step we avoid connecting the chronological data to our own chronological system because ancient writers did not know it. *Second*, we shall present important extrabiblical material, which will help us fix some important events in the Bible and in the Jewish history. It is a well-known fact among scholars that the Assyrian chronological traditions give us the possibility of fixing the reigns of the Assyrian kings into our absolute chronology from 10th century to 7th century BCE.[1] Assyrian documents contain important

---

1. For this see H. Tadmor, 'The Chronology of the First Temple Period: A Presentation and Evaluation of the Sources', in A. Malamat (ed.), *The Age of the Monarchies: Political History* (The World History of the Jewish People, 4/1; Jerusalem: Massada, 1979), pp. 44-60. In her study *Reconstructed Chronology of the Divided Kingdom* (Winona Lake: Eisenbrauns, 2005), M.C. Tetley has attempted to challenge this consensus among scholars. The consequence is that she argues that the beginning of the divided kingdom should be dated to 981 BCE. However, her study is methodologically and argumentatively faulty. Its results must clearly be rejected.

parallels to the events in biblical traditions, and they give us a reliable basis to connect the pre-exilic events of the Bible to our absolute chronology. In addition, Babylonian chronological traditions relate the late pre-exilic and the exilic events of the Bible to the absolute chronology. When we come to the later centuries prior to the Christian era, extra-biblical material is already so imminent that the events can be dated according to a solid chronological basis. *Third*, we shall demonstrate how the biblical and ancient Jewish chronological traditions can be harmonized with extra-biblical material. When needed we shall also clarify how conflicting traditions in the present biblical and Jewish documents have been generated.

The Content of This Book

We shall argue in Chapters 2–5 that there is evidence for the existence of older chronological traditions of the Israelite and Judean kings which have been reworked by biblical writers and later copyists. These older traditions, in turn, are in harmony with the present available extra-biblical documents. This implies that the biblical chronological traditions of the kings of Judah and Israel originated from older annalistic sources or from royal archives.

In Chapter 6 we shall also show that the seventy yearweeks in Dan. 9.24-27 is the starting-point for Josephus when he calculates the chronology of the Jewish people in the postexilic period until the destruction of the Second Temple. This being the case we can conclude that scholars using Josephus's chronology to explain the gap between the exile and the Maccabean period in Dan. 9.24-27 in fact have fallen into a circular argumentation. We shall provide an explanation of how the chronological system in Dan. 9.24-27 should be understood.

In addition, we shall discuss the chronological system of Demetrius which seems to corroborate well with other Jewish chronological traditions of the postexilic period, and which differed from the absolute chronology by about 25/26 years. Thus the basic challenge is to explain the origin of Demetrius's chronology.

See, e.g. the review of G. Galil in *CBQ* 68 (2006), pp. 131-33, and that of L. McFall in *VT* 57 (2007), pp. 574-75. As McFall notes: 'If a new chronology of the Hebrew kings depends crucially on a major redating of Assyrian and Egyptian kings to give it credibility, then it must await the verdict of the experts on those fields before it will find a place in Old Testament studies' (p. 575).

Finally in Chapters 7–8, we shall also discuss the chronological schematizations of the Hebrew Bible which relate to the pre-monarchic period. We put forward arguments that it is impossible to use these schematizations as the basis for the history of Israel but that there are indications that some parts of these chronological traditions may have originated from the pre-exilic period. This in turn raises some interesting questions concerning the tradition blocks which were available for Jerusalemite 'historiographers' before the exile.

Chronology for the Kings of Israel and Judah

In every proposal of biblical chronology the fundamental building blocks consist of synchronisms of the kings of Israel and Judah which are given in the books of Kings. Every reconstructed chronology is built up by three factors: (1) biblical synchronisms, (2) biblical dates of certain events which can be fixed by means of extra-biblical documents as well as (3) references to certain kings of Israel and Judah in the historical events which are accounted in the Assyrian documents and which can be dated accurately. Good examples for case (2) are the destruction of Samaria in 722–720 BCE which is dated to the ninth regnal year of Hosea (2 Kgs 17.6) or to the sixth regnal year of Hezekiah (2 Kgs 18.9-10), or the invasion of Sennacherib in 701 BCE which is dated to the 14th regnal year of Hezekiah (2 Kgs 18.13; Isa 36.1). These two events form a difficult puzzle in biblical chronology because it is easy to see that both biblical datings cannot be simultaneously accurate as they are fixed to the regnal years of Hezekiah, which allows for only eight years between the events, while the Assyrian records indicate that there are about 20 years between them. This illustrates well problems which we have in biblical chronological data. An example which illustrates case (3) is the following: Ahab is mentioned among the opponents of Shalmaneser III in the battle of Qarqar in 853 BCE, and Jehu is mentioned and depicted in the famous Black Obelisk paying tribute to Shalmaneser III in 841 BCE. This being the case the reigns of Ahaziah and Jehoram, which are dated after Ahab's death and before Jehu's rise to power, should be dated between these two years 853 BCE and 841 BCE. By means of biblical synchronisms and relating their data to extrabiblical documents, however, scholars have reconstructed different chronologies for the kings of Israel and Judah. We shall present the most important alternatives.

Albright's Chronology

Albright presented his chronology in a brief article from 1945 and later completed his proposal by presenting two synchronisms between Egypt and Israel/Judah.[2] He notes that it is possible to present only approximate dates. He states, however, that he does not believe that they 'are more than five years wrong'.[3] He actually puts the abbreviation of circa i.e. 'c.' to every regnal period of the kings. We present these figures below without adding 'c.'

Israel		Judah	
Jeroboam I	922–901	Rehoboam	922–915
Nadab	901–900	Abiam	915–913
Baasha	900–877	Asa	913–873
Elah	877–876	Jehoshaphat	873–849
Zimri	876	Jehoram	849–842
Omri	876–869	Ahaziah	842
Ahab	869–850	Athaliah	842–837
Ahaziah	850–849	Joash	837–800
Jehoram	849–842	Amaziah	800–783
Jehu	842–815	Uzziah	783–742
Jehoahaz	815–801	Jotham	750–735
Jehoash	801–786	Ahaz	735–715
Jeroboam II	786–746	Hezekiah	715–687
Zechariah	746–745	Manasseh	687–642
Shallum	745	Amon	642–640
Menahem	745–738	Josiah	640–609
Pekahiah	738–737	Jehoahaz	609
Pekah	737–732	Jehoiakim	609–598
Hosea	732–724	Jeconiah	598
		Zedekiah	598–587

Albright's chronology is based on several corrections he proposes for the biblical data. For example, he suggests that Rehoboam ruled for only eight years (instead of 17 years as in 1 Kgs 14.21)[4], Amaziah for only 18

---

2. W.F. Albright, 'The Chronology of the Divided Monarchy of Israel', *BASOR* 100 (1945), pp. 16-22; Albright, 'Further Light on Synchronisms between Egypt and Asia in the Period 935–685 BC', *BASOR* 130 (1956), pp. 23-27.
3. Albright, 'Chronology', p. 17.
4. Albright argues for his conclusions by referring to 2 Chron. 16.1 according to which 'Baasha was still reigning in the 36th year of Asa'. By using this information Albright concludes that the length of the reign of Rehoboam should be reduced at least eight, probably nine years.

(instead of 29 years as in 2 Kgs 14.2), Uzziah for only 42 years (instead of 52 years as in 2 Kgs 15.2), Menahem for only eight years (instead of 10 years as in 2 Kgs 15.17) etc. Albright also changes the length of the reign of Jehoram of Israel in order to get it – as well as the reign of Ahaziah – to fit between the years 853 BCE (when Ahab battled in Qarqar) and 841 BCE (when Jehu paid tribute).

Albright's method is to connect the biblical data in a straightforward manner to chronological data from the extrabiblical documents. He sees no problem in changing the biblical chronological data without real support in textual evidence. Such methodology is a convincing solution only if we were able to conclude that we do not have accurate chronological data in the books of Kings. It is indeed noteworthy that Albright criticizes the earlier attempt of Begrich to solve chronological problems by writing: 'It is incredible that all these numbers can have been handed down through so many editors and copyists without often becoming corrupt'.[5] As I explained at the beginning of this book my aim is to demonstrate that the synchronisms and other chronological data in the books of Kings form a solid basis for the chronology of the Israelite and Judean kings.

Albright's method to date the beginning of the reigns of Jeroboam I and Rehoboam in 922 BCE was later taken up in another article where he suggested that the beginning of the reign of Shishak should be dated between 937–930 BCE.[6] However, this date is difficult to relate to the present understanding of the Egyptian chronology, according to which Shishak ruled in 945–924 BCE.[7] If Shishak's reign ended in 924 BCE then we should really doubt Albright's self-confidence in changing the chronological data of the Hebrew Bible. For example, by fabricating a new shorter reign of Rehoboam, he postdated the beginning of his reign by nine years.

The basic lines of Albright's chronology are followed in Bright's presentation of the history of Israel. For example, he dates the reigns of Jeroboam I and Rehoboam to 922 BCE and follows Albright's method of dating the reign of Shishak.[8] It is also worth noting that Kuhrt, in her

---

5. Albright, 'The Chronology', p. 17.
6. Albright, 'New Light', pp. 4-8.
7. For this date, see K.A. Kitchen, 'Egypt, History of (Chronology)', *ABD*, II, pp. 322-31.
8. J. Bright, *A History of Israel* (Louisville: Westminster/John Knox Press, 2000); cf. also J.M. Miller and J.H. Hayes, *A History of Ancient Israel and Judah* (Philadelphia: Westminster Press, 1986), pp. 220-21, 226-29. On p. 233 n. 13 Albright's way to date the reign of Shishak is followed.

important survey of the history of the ancient Near East, presents Albright's chronology for the kings of Israel and Judah as one representative example, even though she dates Shishak's reign to 945–924 BCE.[9]

Thiele's Chronology

Thiele's chronology has been regarded as valuable contribution.[10] His most ground-breaking study was his monograph from 1951 but he already developed his ideas in an article written some years earlier. In addition, he has dealt with chronological problems in some other studies.[11]

Israel		Judah	
Jeroboam I	930–909	Rehoboam	930–913
Nadab	909–908	Abiam	913–910
Baasha	908–886	Asa	910–869
Elah	886–885	Jehoshaphat	872–848
Zimri	885	Jehoram	853–841
Omri	885–874	Ahaziah	841
Ahab	874–853	Athaliah	841–835
Ahaziah	853–852	Joash	835–796
Jehoram	852–841	Amaziah	796–767
Jehu	841–814	Uzziah	792–740
Jehoahaz	814–798	Jotham	750–732
Jehoash	798–782	Ahaz	735–715
Jeroboam II	793–753	Hezekiah	715–686
Zechariah	753	Manasseh	697–642
Shallum	752	Amon	642–640
Menahem	752–742	Josiah	640–609
Pekahiah	742–740	Jehoahaz	609
Pekah	752–732	Jehoiakim	609–598
Hosea	732–723	Jeconiah	598–597
		Zedekiah	597–586

9. A. Kuhrt, *The Ancient Near East c. 3000–330 BC: Volumes I & II* (London and New York: Routledge, 1995). In vol. II on p. 468 the chronology of Albright is presented (cf. pp. 456, 466 where the death of Solomon is given c. 930/922); and later in the same volume on p. 624 the date for the reign of Shishak is given.

10. See, e.g., K.A. Strand, 'Thiele's Biblical Chronology as a Corrective for Extrabiblical Dates', *Andrews University Seminary Studies* 34 (1996), pp. 295-317.

11. See E.R. Thiele, *The Mysterious Numbers of the Hebrew Kings: A Reconstruction of the Chronology of the Kingdoms of Israel and Judah* (Chicago: University of Chicago Press, 1951); Thiele, 'The Chronology of the Kings of Judah and Israel', *JNES* 3 (1944), pp. 137-86; Thiele, 'Coregencies and Overlapping Reigns among the Hebrew Kings', *JBL* 93 (1974), pp. 174-200; Thiele, *A Chronology of the Hebrew Kings* (Grand Rapids: Zondervan, 1982).

An important detail in Thiele's proposal is that he argued that the new regnal year in Israel began by the month Nisan, while in Judah that took place in the month Tishri. Another central point in Thiele's system is that it is heavily based on the argument that many conflicting synchronisms in the books of Kings can be solved by an assumption of coregency even though the biblical texts themselves do not indicate such a solution. We shall discuss this explanation model and show that it is more than an argument. An assumption of coregency always implies reconstructed chronological data because the synchronisms in these cases can be calculated in different ways: reference can be made to the year of the king calculated from his total reign (including coregency) or from his sole reign (excluding coregency).

Unlike Albright Thiele does not change the biblical chronological data, and therefore he comes to the conclusion that the reigns of Jeroboam I and Rehoboam should be dated to 930 BCE. This date is in harmony with the date given in 1 Kgs 14.25 according to which Shishak invaded in Palestine in Rehoboam's fifth regnal year. This corresponds to the year 926/925 BCE and can easily be related to the end of the reign of Shishak (945–924 BCE). In our approach we will also emphasize the importance of preserving the chronological data in the books of Kings. Nevertheless, rather than assuming coregencies we seek for other explanations for the chronological problems.

Begrich's and Jepsen's Chronology

One of the earliest chronologies still used in scholarly literature is the proposal made by Begrich[12] which was later taken up and argued for by Jepsen.[13] They present practically identical chronological systems and I have followed here the regnal years given by Jepsen:

Israel		Judah	
Jeroboam I	927–907	Rehoboam	926–910
Nadab	907–906	Abiam	910–908
Baasha	906–883	Asa	908–868

12. J. Begrich, *Die Chronologie der Könige von Israel und Juda und die Quellen des Rahmens der Königsbücher* (Tübingen: Mohr & Siebeck, 1929).
13. A. Jepsen, 'Zur Chronologie der Könige von Israel und Juda', in A. Jepsen and R. Hanhart, *Untersuchungen zur israelitisch-jüdischen Chronologie* (BZAW, 88; Berlin: W. de Gruyter, 1964), pp. 4-48; Jepsen, 'Ein Neuer Fixpunkt für die Chronologie der israelitischen Könige?', *VT* 20 (1970), pp. 359-61.

Elah	883–882	Jehoshaphat	868–847
Zimri	882	Jehoram	847–845
Omri	882–871	Ahaziah	845
Ahab	871–852	Athaliah	845–840
Ahaziah	852–851	Joash	840–801
Jehoram	851–845	Amaziah	801–773
Jehu	845–818	Uzziah	787–736
Jehoahaz	818–802	Jotham	756–741 [759–744]
Jehoash	802–787	Ahaz	741–725 [744–729]
Jeroboam II	787–747	Hezekiah	725–697 [728–700]
Zechariah	747	Manasseh	696–642
Shallum	746	Amon	641–640
Menahem	747–738	Josiah	639–609
Pekahiah	737–736	Jehoahaz	609
Pekah	735–732	Jehoiakim	608–598
Hosea	731–723	Jeconiah	598
		Zedekiah	597–587

In two points Begrich and Jepsen assumed a coregency, namely in the reign of Amaziah when Uzziah was coregent, and in the reign of Uzziah when Jotham was coregent.

The chronology of Begrich and Jepsen gives an interesting proposal for the beginning of the reign of Jehu which is dated in 845 BCE. The proposal is based on the idea that after the reign of Ahab there were kings Ahaziah and Jehoram in both Israel and Judah and, in addition, there are conflicting synchronisms between these kings (see the data in Chapter 2). These conflicting data are explained so that the reign of Jehoram (Israel) was originally shorter and it was later lengthened in order to harmonise conflicting chronological data.[14] This implies that the reigns of Ahaziah and Jehoram in Israel can more easily be dated between 853 BCE (Ahab in Qarqar) and 841 BCE (Jehu paid tribute). We shall return to this attractive solution later in this book.

Another important detail is the reign of Hezekiah, which in Jepsen's chronology is dated to 728 BCE. It differs from the date of 715 BCE in Albright's and Thiele's chronology, which is in harmony with 2 Kgs 18.13 when Sennacherib invaded Judah in Hezekiah's 14th regnal year in 701 BCE. Jepsen's date again is in harmony with 2 Kgs 18.9-10, according to which Samaria was destroyed in Hezekiah's 6th regnal year. Finally, we can note that Jepsen dates the beginning of the reigns of Jeroboam I and Rehoboam slightly later than Thiele. This is due to the fact that biblical data allow for two different conclusions as far the length of the reign of Ahab is concerned (20 years or 22 years).

14. Jepsen, 'Zur Chronologie', pp. 39-41.

Hayes' and Hooker's Chronology

An alternative worthy of mention is also Hayes' and Hooker's proposal.[15] They argue that the month Marheshvan began the regnal year in Israel, whereas Tishri was the first month in Judah. However, in Judah at the time of Josiah's reform, the Tishri calendar was later substituted by the Nisan-calendar.

Israel		Judah	
Jeroboam I	927–906	Rehoboam	926–910
Nadab	905–904	Abiam	909–907
Baasha	903–882[880]	Asa	906–878[866]
Elah	881–880	Jehoshaphat	877–853
Zimri	880	Jehoram	852–841
Omri	879–869	Ahaziah	840
Ahab	868–854	Athaliah	839–833
Ahaziah	853–852	Joash	832–803[793]
Jehoram	851–840	Amaziah	802–786[774]
Jehu	839–822	Uzziah	785–760[734]
Jehoahaz	821–805	Jotham	759–744
Jehoash	804–789	Ahaz	743–728
Jeroboam II	788–748	Hezekiah	727–699
Zechariah	747	Manasseh	698–644
Shallum	746	Amon	643–642
Menahem	746–737	Josiah	641–610
Pekahiah	736–735	Jehoahaz	609
Pekah	734–731	Jehoiakim	608–598
Hosea	730–722	Jeconiah	598–597
		Zedekiah	596–586

The chronological table reveals some peculiarities. First of all the reign of Ahab is much shorter than the biblical data indicate (20 or 22 years), namely only 15 years. Hayes and Hooker explain this by noting boldly (p. 28): 'Because of the difficulties involved in synchronizing a reign of twenty-two years, we have assumed that Ahab reigned for fifteen years'. Ahab's last year began in 854, in month Marheshvan and it ended in 853, so that Ahab had time to battle in Qarqar against Shalmaneser III as recorded in the Assyrian royal inscriptions. Nevertheless, this dating of the reign of Ahab implies that he had no time to struggle against Arameans as found in 1 Kings 22, according to which Ahab also died in

---

15. J.H. Hayes and P.K. Hooker, *A New Chronology for the Kings of Israel and Judah and its Implications for the Biblical History and Literature* (Atlanta: John Knox Press, 1988).

1. Introduction

this battle. Therefore Hayes and Hooker suggest that the name of Ahab has been added later in 1 Kings 22 (p. 29).

Another unusual proposal is that Jehu was not king when he paid tribute to Shalmaneser III in 841 BCE. He began to rule only two years later in 839 BCE. Hayes and Hooker fix the beginning of the reigns of Jeroboam I and Rehoboam later than Thiele by arguing that the dates are 'based on calculating backward from later kings' reigns which can be determined with reasonable exactitude' (p. 18). As we shall see later in this book we also follow this basic principle of 'calculating backward' but our chronology differs in this point from that of Hayes and Hooker. It should be also noted that even Hayes and Hooker suggest that conflicting synchronisms can be solved by arguing for coregencies.

Hughes's Chronology

The chronology of Hughes is an example of independent scholarly work. He considers all biblical chronological data and is therefore an important source for everyone who is interested to get an overall picture of the biblical chronology.[16]

Israel		Judah	
Jeroboam I	937–913	Rehoboam	937–921
Nadab	913–912	Abiam	921–916
Baasha	912–889	Asa	916–876
Elah	889–888	Jehoshaphat	876–852
Zimri	888	Jehoram	852–842
Omri	888–877	Ahaziah	842
Ahab	877–854	Athaliah	842–836
Ahaziah	854–853	Joash	836–799
Jehoram	853–842	Amaziah	799–772
Jehu	842–816	Uzziah	772–?747
Jehoahaz	816–800	Jotham	?747–737
Jehoash	800–785	Ahaz	737–722
Jeroboam II	785–745	Hezekiah	722–694
Zechariah	745	Manasseh	694–640
Shallum	745	Amon	640–639
Menahem	745–736	Josiah	639–609
Pekahiah	736–735	Jehoahaz	609
Pekah	735–732	Jehoiakim	608–598
Hosea	732–724	Jeconiah	598
		Zedekiah	598–587

16. J. Hughes, *Secrets of the Times: Myth and History in Biblical Chronology* (JSOTSup, 66; Sheffield: Sheffield Academic Press, 1990).

Hughes gives very early date for the reigns of Jeroboam I and Rehoboam by putting them in 937 BCE. Such an early date is hardly possible even though Hughes argues that one does not really know the exact date of the invasion of Shishak. Hughes dates Shishak's reign to 951–930 BCE.

It is worth noting that Hughes's chronological table indicates the regnal year which began in the autumn and ended the following year before the autumn. This being the case Ahab's last regnal year began in autumn 854 BCE and lasted to the summer in 853 BCE when he, according to the inscription of the Assyrian king Shalmaneser III, battled in Qarqar. This in turn, makes Hughes argue that 'there are good reasons for doubting the historical accuracy of 1 Kings 22' (p. 187) which recounts Ahab's death in his battle against Arameans.

A peculiar feature in Hughes's proposal is that the reign of Hezekiah is fixed to the years 722–694 and this dating correlates neither with the synchronism in 2 Kgs 18.9-10 (the destruction of Samaria in Hezekiah's 6th regnal year) nor with the synchronism in 2 Kgs 18.13 (the invasion of Sennacherib in Hezekiah's 14th regnal year). Hughes argues that '*neither* synchronism is historically authentic' (p. 212). In his opinion Isa. 14.28-32 gives us a possibility to date the death of Ahaz to 722 BCE (pp. 212-18).

Galil's Chronology

The newest proposal of the chronology of the kings of Israel and Judah is presented by Galil.[17] Especially noteworthy is Galil's article from 2010 where argued that according to the Deuteronomist the period from the establishment of the First Temple until its destruction lasted for 400 years.[18]

Israel		Judah	
Jeroboam I	931/30–909	Rehoboam	931/30–913
Nadab	909–908	Abiam	914–910
Baasha	908–885	Asa	911–870
Elah	885–884	Jehoshaphat	870–845
Zimri	884	Jehoram	851–843/42
Omri	884–873	Ahaziah	843/2–842/1

17. G. Galil, *The Chronology of the Kings of Israel and Judah* (Studies in the History and Culture of the Ancient Near East, 9; Leiden: Brill, 1996).

18. G. Galil, 'Dates and Calendars', in A. Lemaire and B. Halpern (eds.), *The Books of Kings: Sources, Composition, Historiography and Reception* (VTSup, 129; Leiden: Brill, 2010), pp. 427-43.

Ahab	873–852	Athaliah	842/1–835
Ahaziah	852–851	Jehoash	(842/1)–802/1
Jehoram	851–842/1	Amaziah	805/4–776/5
Jehu	842/1–815/4	Uzziah	788/7–736/5
Jehoahaz	819–804/3	Jotham	758/7–742/1
Jehoash	805–790	Ahaz	742/1–726
Jeroboam II	790–750/49	Hezekiah	726–697/6
Zechariah	750/49	Manasseh	697/6–642/1
Shallum	749	Amon	642/1–640/39
Menahem	749–738	Josiah	640/39–609
Pekahiah	738–736	Jehoahaz	609
Pekah	(750?)–732/31	Jehoiakim	609–598
Hosea	732/1–722	Jeconiah	598–597
		Zedekiah	597–586

It becomes clear from this chronological table that even Galil's proposal allows several overlapping reigns, which he explains with the aid of coregencies (as Thiele before him). An important detail in this proposal is the fixing of the reign of Hezekiah, and which is based on the view that the fate of Samaria accounted in 2 Kgs 17.1-6 telescopes two historical events, the attack of Shalmaneser V (in 722 BCE) and the exile of the people of Samaria which took place in the reign of Sargon II i.e. in 720 BCE. Therefore the ultimate destruction of Samaria was regarded to have taken place only in 720 BCE which, according to Galil's reconstruction, corresponds to Hezekiah's 6th regnal year as indicated in 2 Kgs 18.9-10 (pp. 83-97).

Four Preliminary Questions

This survey actualizes four important methodological questions related to the chronology of the kings of Israel and Judah: (1) When did the royal new year begin? There are two alternatives: in the autumn (Tishri) and in the spring (Nisan). (2) How were the years of enthronement calculated? Was there an accession-year; i.e. was the following year after the year of the enthronement calculated as the first official regnal year? Or was a non-accession-year system followed; i.e. the enthroning year was taken as the first official regnal year? (3) In which way was the system of co-regency practiced? (4) How should text-critical variants between ancient manuscripts be evaluated?

The New Year

There is evidence that the official regnal years of the Judean kings were reckoned from Tishri to Tishri but that the numbers of months were calculated according to the Nisan calendar. This bipartite calendar system was due to the fact that originally the months were mentioned by name (as, for example, in the Assyrian and Babylonian documents) but later replaced with their numbers when the Nisan calendar was imposed as a result of the Babylonian influence.[19] That the names of the months could be called according to numbers even though they do not correspond to the actual order of the months in the year-system is seen also in our Western traditions: September, October, November and December. The following facts support the view that the regnal years were calculated from Tishri to Tishri:

1. The Tishri calendar system was applied by the ancient Canaanites as the famous Gezer Calendar shows.[20] Similar conclusions can be derived from biblical texts. Exodus 23.14-17; 34.18-23 refer to the autumnal festival of ingathering at the 'going out' of the year or the 'turn' of the year.[21] Even sabbatical years and jubilees began in Tishri (Exod. 23.10-11; Deut. 15 and Lev. 25).
2. 1 Kgs 6.1, 37-38 reports that Solomon built the Temple in seven years beginning in the month of Ziv (i.e. the second month) of Solomon 4 and finished it in the month of Bul (i.e. the eighth month) of Solomon 11. If the Nisan calendar is followed, then

---

19. In the Old Testament the Nisan calendar was used in, for example, Ezekiel, the Pentateuch and Chronicles. The names of the months are as follows (listed according to Tishri-year): 7. Tishri, 8. Marheshvan, 9. Kislev, 10. Tebet, 11. Shebat, 12. Adar, 1. Nisan, 2. Iyyar, 3. Sivan, 4. Tammuz, 5. Ab, 6. Elul. See J. Finegan, *Handbook of Biblical Chronology: Principles of Time Reckoning in the Ancient World and Problems of Chronology in the Bible* (Peabody: Hendrickson Publishers, rev. edn, 1998), pp. 76-80. If this is the case then Jer. 36.22 which refers to the winter time and to the ninth month does not prove the Nisan-calendar-system in Judah (cf. Galil, *Chronology of the Kings of Israel and Judah*, pp. 9-10). The text only proves that the name of the months have been substituted by numbers according to Nisan-calendar.

20. See the interpretation of the Gezer Calendar in S. Talmon, *King, Cult and Calendar in Ancient Israel: Collected Studies* (Jerusalem: Magnes Press, The Hebrew University, 1986), pp. 89-112.

21. D.J.A. Clines ('The Evidence for an Autumnal New Year in Pre-exilic Israel Reconsidered', *JBL* 93 [1974], pp. 22-40) has emphasized that 'the end of the year' in these cases must not mean 'the end of the calendar year'. However, in my view the most natural way to read this textual evidence is that the calendar year in ancient Israel was interconnected with agricultural seasons.

its construction took seven and a half years which implies that the Temple was built in eight years. The Tishri calendar gives us six and half years which corresponds well to 'seven years'.[22]
3. According to 2 Kings 23 Josiah's reformation and the festival of the Passover are dated to Josiah's 18th year. The Deuteronomistic editor postulates that Josiah succeeded in implementing all his reforms in a mere two weeks – which would be the case if the Nisan calendar was followed. However, if the Tishri calendar was in use then Josiah had approximately six months to introduce his reforms before the Passover festival on 14 Nisan.[23]
4. Finally we can mention the fact that the Rosh Hashanah feast has been assigned to Tishri (Lev. 23). There is no good explanation for this if the Nisan calendar was followed in Judah. After all, the Babylonian New Year festival was celebrated in Nisan. Therefore the only relevant conclusion is that the Tishri calendar was in use in Israel/Judah before the exile, and thus the Nisan calendar was adopted only during the Babylonian exile.

Some scholars have emphasized that the use of the Tishri calendar in Judah also receives support from the book of Ezekiel. They argue that according to the book of Ezekiel the siege of Jerusalem would have lasted about three years. According to Ezek. 24.1 it began 'in the ninth year, in the tenth month on the tenth day' which is often connected with the tenth day (= 10) of the tenth month (= X) in the ninth year (= 9) of Jeconiah's captivity (= Jeconiah 9.X.10). In that case, according to Ezek.

---

22. See Thiele, *Mysterious Numbers*, pp. 30-31. However, note here Clines's counter arguments ('Autumnal New Year in Pre-exilic Israel', pp. 30-32). Clines regards it as possible that 'seven years' have been calculated from Solomon's 11th regnal year (when the Temple was completed) minus Solomon's 4th regnal year (when the fundament of the Temple was established). However, the Hebrew system of calculating was that the length of the period between the days/years x and y is y-x+1. This is well illustrated by the New Testament evidence according to which Jesus arose on the third day i.e. on Sunday when he died on Friday.

23. Cf. Begrich, *Chronologie*, pp. 68-69; Thiele, *Mysterious Numbers*, p. 32. Hayes and Hooker (*New Chronology*) postulated that the Nisan Calendar was introduced in Judah during Josiah's reform. Even Begrich (*Chronologie*, pp. 70-90) argues that the Nisan-calendar was adopted about 620 BCE in Judah. Jepsen ('Zur Chronologie', pp. 4-48) and Galil (*Chronology of the Kings of Israel and Judah*, pp. 9-10) argue that the Nisan-calendar was followed in Judah. I shall propose that Jeconiah's exile introduced the Nisan calendar in Judah but we can still see two parallel chronological systems: Tishri calendar (in conjunction of the reign of Zedekiah) and Nisan-calendar (in conjunction of the reign of Jeconiah) in the book of Ezekiel. See Chapter 4.

33.21, the prophet received a message to this effect on Jeconiah 12.X.5. According to 2 Kings 25, the siege began on Zedekiah 9.X.10 and the city was captured on Zedekiah 11.IV.9. If, however, the Nisan calendar was followed for Zedekiah's official regnal years, then the siege would have lasted for about 18 months and Ezekiel would only have had word of it one and half years later, which seems improbable. On the other hand, if the Tishri calendar was followed then between Tebet 10 in Zedekiah 9 (Zedekiah 9.X.10) and Ab 7 in Zedekiah 11 (Zedekiah 11.IV.9) there are about 30 months which corresponds more closely to the chronological data in the book of Ezekiel, where the years of Jeconiah's captivity were reckoned according to the Babylonian system, i.e. according to the Nisan-calendar.[24] Nevertheless, Kutsch has argued that the date in Ezek. 24.1 is formally different from other dates in the book of Ezekiel and therefore probably a later editorial work. He argues that it should refer to Zedekiah 9.X.10 instead of Jeconiah 9.X.10.[25] This implies that this date cannot be used as an argument for the use of the Tishri calendar.[26]

Hayes and Hooker have argued that the Nisan calendar was introduced in Judah during the reform of Josiah.[27] Their argument is based on the assumption that the months are numerated according to the Nisan-calendar – a view which we have also accepted in this study. As an example they refer to Jer. 36.22-23 – according to which the scroll of Jeremiah was burned in the winter palace in the ninth month – and argue that this must have taken place during winter i.e. in the month of Kislev. Our opinion is that using numbers for the months was a system adopted by the Judeans during the Babylonian exile and that consequently they applied this system in biblical scrolls. Only in a few cases were the older names of the Canaanite months preserved (1 Kgs 6.1, 37-38; 8.2). Nevertheless, this new system of enumeration did not relocate the place of the New Year from Tishri to Nisan – something which is still visible in the cultic calendar of the later Priestly source (Lev. 25). This being the

---

24. See A. Malamat, 'The Last Kings of Judah and the Fall of Jerusalem', *IEJ* 18 (1968), pp. 137-56, esp. 150.

25. E. Kutsch, *Die Chronologischen Daten des Ezechielbuches* (OBO, 62; Freiburg: Universitätsverlag, 1985), pp. 61-63.

26. It is worth noting that W. Zimmerli (*Ezekiel 1* [Hermeneia; Philadelphia: Fortress Press, 1979], p. 498) argues that the date is Jeconiah 9.X.10, which in his opinion is the same as Zedekiah 9.X.10. He dates this event to January 15, 588 corresponding to Nebuchadnezzar's 17th regnal year by referring to R.A. Parker and W.H. Dubberstein, *Babylonian Chronology 626 B.C.–A.D. 75* (Brown University Studies, 19; Providence: Brown University Press, 1956).

27. Hayes and Hooker, *New Chronology*, p. 86.

case, Jer. 36.22 does not show anything other than the book of Jeremiah having received its final form in the exilic or postexilic time when the Babylonian system for months was adopted.

Accession-year or Non-accession-year System

It is a well-known fact that in ancient Near Eastern documents the year of enthronement was not always calculated as the first regnal year of the king. Therefore, scholars have discussed whether accession-year or non-accession-year system was practiced in ancient Israel and Judah.[28] It is clear that the non-accession-year system is supported by many synchronisms in the books of Kings. For example, Abiam became king in Jeroboam's 18th regnal year and reigned three years (1 Kgs 15.1-2). Asa, the son of Abiam became king in Jeroboam's 20th regnal year (1 Kgs 15.9-10). Thus we received the following synchronisms (by using formulas such as Abiam 1 = Jeroboam 18 meaning that Abiam became king in Jeroboam's 18th regnal year and the first regnal year of Abiam corresponds to Jeroboam's 18th regnal year; formula Abiam 0 = Jeroboam 18 demonstrates that Abiam became king in Jeroboam's 18th regnal year and his official first year is identical with Jeroboam's 19th regnal year etc.):

> Abiam 1 = Jeroboam 18
> Abiam 2 = Jeroboam 19
> Abiam 3 = Asa 1 = Jeroboam 20

A similar argument is also valid for the two years' reign of Nadav. He became king in Asa's second regnal year (1 Kgs 15.25) and Basha after him became king in Asa's third regnal year:

> Asa 2 = Nadab 1
> Asa 3 = Nadab 2 = Baasha 1

According to Thiele, the non-accession-year system would have been applied in Israel during the period from Jeroboam I to Ahaziah, while in Judah the accession-year system was applied for the same period. He demonstrates this by comparing the lengths of the reigns between Judah and Israel in the following way:[29]

---

28. See the detailed discussion in Thiele, *Mysterious Numbers*, pp. 19-29; Thiele, *A Chronology of the Hebrew Kings*, pp. 16-22. Thiele argues that accession and non-accession year systems varied in Judah and Israel.

29. Thiele, *A Chronology of the Hebrew Kings*, p. 18.

Judah		Israel		
Rehoboam	17	Jeroboam	22	21 (actual years)
Abiam	3	Nadab	2	1
Asa	41	Baasha	24	23
Jehoshaphat	18	Elah	2	1
		Omri	12	11
		Ahab	22	21
		Ahaziah	2	1
Total:	79		86	79

At first sight this way of calculating regnal years seems to be convincing. However, a closer look reveals how problematic Thiele's calculation is. *First* of all Thiele's calculation does not prove the validity of the accession-year system in Judah and the non-accession-year system in Israel. It only shows one theoretical mathematical possibility of calculating the sums of the lengths of the reigns of the Judean and Israelite kings so that their sums are identical. *Second*, we have already demonstrated that synchronisms in 1 Kgs 15.1-2, 9-10 indicate the accession-year system in Judah. At the beginning of Chapter 2 we shall demonstrate that there are other problems in chronological details of biblical synchronisms which cannot be related to accession-year or non-accession-year systems. The *third* point is that according to 1 Kgs 14.20 Jeroboam reigned for 22 years. However, the synchronisms in 1 Kgs 15.9-10, 25 give us reason to argue that Jeroboam reigned for only 21 years. And finally, *fourth*, synchronisms in 1 Kgs 22.41-42, 52 imply that Jehoshaphat's 17th regnal year was Ahab's 20th regnal year when Ahaziah became king in Israel. This would allow only a 20 year reign for Ahab. This being the case, Thiele's calculation does not prove an accession-year and non-accession-year systems for Judah and Israel respectively. Rather his mathematical calculation is accidentally accurate, and biblical synchronisms themselves disprove Thiele's hypothesis.

One may argue that the accession-year system could explain the synchronisms from the later period, for example, in the case of the reign of Uzziah. We find the following three synchronisms: Uzziah 39 = Menahem became king (2 Kgs 15.17); Uzziah 50 = Pekahiah became king (2 Kgs 15.23) and Uzziah 52 = Pekah became king (2 Kgs 15.27). These synchronisms can be used to generate the following table according to accession-year-system and non-accession-year system:

1. Introduction

Uzziah 39	= Menahem 0	= Menahem 1
Uzziah 40	= Menahem 1	= Menahem 2
Uzziah 48	= Menahem 9	= Menahem 10
Uzziah 49	= Menahem 10	= Menahen 11
Uzziah 50	= Menahem 11 = Pekahiah 0	= Menahem 12 = Pekahiah 1
Uzziah 51	= Pekahiah 1	= Pekahiah 2
Uzziah 52	= Pekahiah 2 = Pekah 0	= Pekahiah 3 = Pekah 1

It becomes apparent that the 10-year reign of Menahem does not fit in well with any of the systems and in the non-accession-year system the two-year reign of Pekahiah is also problematic. Even though the accession-year system seems to accord better for the Israelite kings during this period, we cannot speak about exact correspondence. Therefore, we must be careful not to assume a system which *de facto* does not function well for the biblical material. The basic problem is that synchronisms are in tension with each other, and we must attempt to explain how the conflicting synchronisms have been generated. In this study *we shall apply a non-accession-year system for both Judah and Israel* and be open to the possibility of applying an accession-year-system as an explanation model for certain periods of biblical chronology.

We shall see that the accession-year system seems to receive support from chronological details concerning the late Judean kings prior to the exilic period i.e. during the period when Samaria had already been destroyed and there was no possibility to present synchronisms between the Israelite and Judean kings. We shall return to this question in Chapters 3–4.

Co-regency as an Explanation Model

Scholars have argued that co-regency may often be used to solve conflicting synchronisms in the books of Kings.[30] That co-regency has been

---

30. See e.g. Thiele, *Mysterious Numbers*, pp. 35-37; Thiele, *Chronology of the Hebrew Kings*; J. Gray, *1 and 2 Kings: A Commentary* (OTL; London: SCM, 1970); Galil, *Chronology of the Kings of Israel and Judah*, p. 10; G. Larsson, 'The Chronology of the Kings of Israel and Judah as a System', *ZAW* 114 (2002), pp. 224-35. There are many scholars who consider the whole concept of coregency as unjustified (the only exception is 2 Kgs 15.5). See, e.g., Begrich, *Chronologie*; Jepsen, 'Zur Chronologie'; K.T. Andersen, 'Die Chronologie der Könige von Israel und Juda', *ST* 23 (1969), pp. 69-114; Andersen, 'Noch einmal: Die Chronologie der Königen von Israel und Juda', *SJOT* 3 (1989), pp. 1-45. Even Hayes and Hooker (*New Chronology*, p. 12) deny co-regencies but their proposal nevertheless contains several overlaps. For this critical evaluation of Hayes and Hooker see Hughes, *Secrets of the Times*, p. 99 n. 2.

applied in ancient Near East is easy to demonstrate.[31] More complicated is the question in which way co-regencies have influenced the chronological traditions in the biblical documents. Even though there are some cases where double-dating was practiced in ancient Near Eastern documents, we have no example of such dating in the Hebrew Bible. Therefore, any solution which refers to co-regencies is problematic in two respects. *First*, the biblical synchronisms contain apparent problems which cannot be solved by referring to co-regencies. There is a risk that one sees co-regency in cases where we should simply use other arguments to solve problems in the biblical chronological system. *Secondly*, co-regency is mathematically a very powerful tool and can be used in different ways to solve problems in synchronisms. Na'aman, who in principle is not against co-regencies, considers carefully four important cases concerning co-regencies. These cases indicate that scholars have different possibilities to calculate the co-regency and its overlapping with the regnal years of the ruler:[32]

1. 'Does the age of a king when he ascended the throne point to his commencement of co-regency, or to the beginning of his sole reign?'
2. 'Are the years counted for a king designate his sole rule exclusive of co-regency, or rather his entire term of kingship including the years overlapping with those of his father?'
3. 'Does the synchronism for the accession refer to the beginning of the co-regency, or to the commencement of his sole reign?'
4. 'Are the years of the neighbouring king in this synchronism counted from the commencement of his co-regency, or from the start of his sole reign?'

In his article on coregencies Thiele emphasizes how 'the numbers in Kings have proven themselves to be remarkably accurate'.[33] He mentions that in the chronological data of the books of Kings there are exactly 152 years from Ahab to Sennacherib's attack on Judah which corresponds to the data in Assyrian inscriptions, and in a similar way he emphasizes that the chronological data from the accession of Jehu to the fall of Samaria both in the biblical text and Assyrian inscriptions correspond to each other (= 118 years).[34] However, these two claims are not valid for the

31. See the evidence in Egyptian documents in W.J. Murnane, *Ancient Egyptian Coregencies* (SAOC, 40; Chicago: The Oriental Institute, 1977).
32. N. Na'aman, 'Historical and Chronological Notes on the Kingdoms of Israel and Judah in the Eight Century B.C.', *VT* 36 (1986), pp. 71-92, esp. 85.
33. Thiele, 'Coregencies, esp. p. 198.
34. Thiele, 'Coregencies', pp. 198-99.

biblical data itself, but rather only after Thiele has modified it by his theories about coregencies and overlapping reigns. Thiele's argumentation in that article contains some serious problems.

Thiele dates the reigns of the following kings in the following way (note several overlapping reigns):[35]

Menahem	752–742/41	Uzziah	791/90–740/39
Pekahiah	742/41–740/39	Jotham	750–732/31
Pekah	752–732/31	Ahaz	735–716/15
Hoshea	732/31–723/22	Hezekiah	716/15–687/86

According to Thiele, Pekah was a rival ruler at the time of Menahem and Pekahiah. From the chronological tables we can observe that Jotham became king in Pekahiah 2 (2 Kgs 15.32) and Ahaz became king in Pekah 17 (2 Kgs 16.1). Thiele is then faced with the problem of explaining the following synchronisms:

Ahaz 12	= Hoshea 1 (2 Kgs 17.1)
Hoshea 3	= Hezekiah 1 (2 Kgs 18.1)
Hezekiah 6	= Conquest of Samaria (2 Kgs 18.10)

Thiele solves the problem by assuming that an editor shifted Pekah's 20-year reign to begin only in 740/39 i.e. after Pekahiah's reign. Therefore Pekah's reign would be 740/39–720/19 and Hoshea's 720/19–711/10. So, assuming that Ahaz became king in 732/31, Thiele fixes the following synchronisms:

Ahaz 12	= 720/19	= Hoshea 1
Hoshea 3	= 716	= Hezekiah 1
Hezekiah 6	= 711/10	= Conquest of Samaria (2 Kgs 18.10)

Thiele thus first joins Jotham's and Ahaz' reigns with our modern chronology. He then shifts the beginning of Pekah's reign to 740/39, assuming that the beginnings of Jotham's and Ahaz's reigns do not need to be shifted accordingly, even though the beginnings of these reigns are reckoned according to Pekah's reign (Jotham 1 = Pekah 2 and Ahaz 1 = Pekah 17). In fact what Thiele thus assumes is that the beginnings of Jotham's and Ahaz's reigns are determined by some other method than with the aid of Pekah's reign. But how? Certainly not with our modern chronology. Thiele ought first to find some other way of determining the reigns of Jotham and Ahaz if he is to assume that the commencements of their reigns do not change when that of Pekah does.

---

35. See his argumentation in Thiele, 'Coregencies', pp. 194-99.

The regnal years which Na'aman in his article gives to Judean and Israelite kings cannot explain all problems in the biblical synchronisms in 2 Kgs 14.23; 15.1; 17.1. Even though Thiele's construction finds a solution to the synchronism in 2 Kgs 14.23, he nevertheless cannot use the co-regency-argument to solve the synchronisms in 2 Kgs 15.1; 17.1. This indicates that there are more fundamental problems in biblical synchronisms and therefore a reference to co-regency may simply be a wrong way to solve such problems. The discussion becomes even more hypothetical when reference is made to the archaeological evidence such as Samaria Ostraca and the idea of co-regency is imposed on that material.[36]

This being the case, we must first carefully consider all problems involved in biblical synchronism, before we begin to use the powerful explanation of model of co-regency. In this study we shall first deal with conflicting biblical synchronisms from other relevant viewpoints. We shall ask whether they can be the result of different traditions transmitted in biblical sources or whether they are the result of editorial reworking. Of course in those cases where biblical tradition clearly indicates that co-regency was an option it is meaningful to use this explanation. Such a case is mentioned, for example, in 2 Kgs 15.5 and we shall deal with this case of Jotham's co-regency more closely later in this study.

Text-critical Considerations Combined with other Speculations

One important aspect in reconstruction of the biblical chronology has been textual criticism.[37] The Septuagint manuscripts contain a lot of variations but many of them must be evaluated simply as attempts to improve the Hebrew text. A translator has realized internal tensions in the synchronisms and wanted to harmonize texts.[38] Therefore, we must

---

36. See e.g. the contrived theory of W.H. Shea ('The Date and Significance of the Samaria Ostraca', *IEJ* 27 [1977], pp. 16-27). Na'aman ('Kingdoms of Israel and Judah', pp. 80-81) has rightly shown the weaknesses of this theory.

37. A basic study on the chronological details in the Septuagint tradition is J.D. Shenkel, *Chronology and Recensional Development in the Greek Text of Kings* (Cambridge, MA: Harvard University Press, 1968). Shenkel argues that the Septuagint tradition is superior to the MT data. This view has been rightly criticized by scholars. See, in particular, D.W. Gooding's review on Shenkel's study in *JTS* 21 (1970), pp. 118-31. See also A.R. Green, 'The Chronology of the Last Days of Judah: Two Apparent Discrepancies', *JBL* 101 (1982), pp. 57-73.

38. Concerning text-critical variants between the MT and LXX see, in particular, Begrich, *Chronologie*; Galil, *Chronology of the Kings of Israel and Judah*.

1. Introduction

respect here the text-critical rule *lectio difficilior potior* which means that when the synchronism is in tension with other synchronisms there is a tendency in textual transmission process to change the text and eliminate the tension.

Text-critical considerations can also be presented in conjunction with other speculations concerning co-regencies or accession-year and non-accession-year systems. A good example is Schedl's article.[39] For the period from Jehu to Samaria's destruction he proposes some text-critical emendations for biblical chronological data and, in addition, presupposes three co-regencies with certain lengths (not given in the Bible) and assumes that only in some cases should the accession-year system be applied, and in these cases argues that the chronological data of the kings of Israel and Judah can be put in harmony:[40]

Israel: from Jehu to the destruction of Samaria
The sum of the lengths of the reigns:

28 + 17 + 16 + (41) + 10 + 2 + (20) + 9		= 143
Corrections:	Pekah's reign only 10 years	= -10
	Co-regency of Jerobeam	= -11
	Three non-accession-years	= -3
The sum of years in total		= 119

Judah: from Athaliah to the destruction of Samaria in Hezekiah's sixth year
The sum of the lengths of the reigns:

6 + 40 + (29) + (52) + (16) + (16) + 6		= 165
Corrections:	Ahaz' reign endured for only 6 years	= -10
	Co-regency of Uzziah	= -23
	Co-regency of Jotham	= -11
	Two non-accession-years	= -2
The sum of years in total		
		= 119

It is easy to see how important role a modern exegete plays here when Schedl changes the numbers of the kings of Israel and Judah by speculating text-critical emendations and the lengths of co-regencies and assuming non-accession-years in some cases. As far as I can see this kind of argumentation is so arbitrary that it is no wonder if some scholars argue that it is not possible to present any valid reconstruction of the biblical chronology.

---

39. C. Shedl, 'Textkritische Bemerkungen zu den Synchronismen der Könige von Israel und Juda', *VT* 12 (1962), pp. 88-119.
40. See the table in Schedl, 'Synchronismen der Könige', p. 99.

Another example of arbitrary argumentation is Albright's article to which we already have referred.[41] He notes that the lengths of all Judean kings from Athaliah to Ahaz were textually corrupt, but also maintains that 'once the numbers were included in the text of the great work of the Deuteronomist, they were transmitted by copyists with astonishing accuracy'.[42] Albright's chronology is an example of the argumentation of how a biblical scholar can fabricate history by manipulating biblical sources.[43]

Summing up we may conclude that it is important to first detect problems of biblical synchronisms and avoid using both co-regencies and textual corrections based on the Septuagint [sic] as *deus ex machina* solutions.[44]

---

41. See especially Albright, 'Chronology of the Divided Monarchy'. See further Albright, 'New Light from Egypt'; Albright, 'Further Light on Synchronisms between Egypt and Asia in the Period 935–685 BC', *BASOR* 130 (1956), pp. 23-27.

42. Albright, 'Chronology of the Divided Monarchy', p. 19 n. 12.

43. See further the justified criticism against Albright in Hughes, *Secrets of the Times*, pp. 108-109.

44. Problematic is also the study of K. Stenring, *The Enclosed Garden* (Stockholm: Almqvist & Wiksell, 1966). He tried to demonstrate that there were three different systems of calculation in biblical data. G. Larsson ('The Chronology of the Kings of Israel and Judah'; Larsson, 'Septuagint versus Massoretic Chronology', *ZAW* 114 [2002], pp. 511-21) has argued for this system. The problem of Stenring's sophisticated solution is that ancient writers were incapable of using exact astronomical knowledge and the biblical synchronisms do not provide coherent data for us.

2

THE CHRONOLOGICAL DATA OF THE ISRAELITE AND JUDEAN KINGS

In this chapter we shall discuss the chronological data which is given in the book of Kings. We shall deal with three important topics: (1) Can we assume that the chronological data given in the books of Kings originates from royal archives? (2) The content of the chronological data of the books of Kings. (3) In which way do the extrabiblical documents challenge the chronological data in the books of Kings? These three topics are essential background for our further discussion with this data.

Synchronisms and Royal Archives

The essential question in Chapters 2–4 is whether it can be argued that biblical synchronisms are based on the reliable sources which originate from Israelite and Judean royal archives. *Prima facie* we must be open for this possibility because the books of Kings indicate that their writers used older sources. There are many references to the sources which can be regarded as annals:[1] 1 Kgs 11.41; 14.19, 29; 15.7, 23, 31; 16.5, 14, 20, 27; 22.39, 46; 2 Kgs 1.18; 8.23; 10.34; 12.20; 13.8, 12; 14.15, 18, 28; 15.6, 11, 15, 21, 26, 31, 36; 16.19; 20.20; 21.17, 25; 23.28; 24.5. This list of sources gives us reason to think that the Deuteronomist used older written sources when he composed the history of kingdoms of Judah and Israel. Consequently there is reason to ask whether biblical synchronisms are also connected with these older royal archives. My aim in this book is to show that this really is the case. I believe that we can demonstrate this by clarifying argumentation and thus avoid solutions which are based on many variables which a scholar can change by his own will.

---

1. For this characterization 'annals' see N.P. Lemche, *Ancient Israel: A New History of Israelite Society* (Sheffield: Sheffield Academic Press, 1988), p. 58.

Instead of such *ad hoc* argumentation we shall present *the reasoning* which led to the synchronisms in the books of Kings. We shall see that we can often assume that the synchronisms are based on data of older royal archives which contained accurate synchronisms, but sometimes we must also clarify reasoning which led to synchronisms which are in conflict with other material in the books of Kings.

The Biblical Synchronisms of the Israelite and Judean Kings

The most detailed chronological system in the Bible consists of the synchronisms between the kings of Israel and the kings of Judah. All discussions concerning the biblical chronology must begin with these data because this period of biblical chronology can be related to chronological data in Assyrian and Babylonian documents which, in turn, can be fixed to our modern chronology. We shall now present all available synchronisms of the books of Kings. The formula Abiam 1 [3] = Jeroboam 18 means that Abiam became king in Jeroboam's 18th year and Abiam reigned three years. The footnotes contain more information about these synchronisms as well as ancient variants in textual traditions and should thus be consulted in order to properly understand the argument presented here:[2]

Jeroboam [22]	1 Kgs 14.20
Reheabeam [17]	1 Kgs 14.21
Rehabeam 5 = Shishak's invasion	1 Kgs 14.25
Abiam 1 [3] = Jeroboam 18	1 Kgs 15.1-2
Asa 1 [41] = Jeroboam 20	1 Kgs 15.9-10[3]
Asa 2 = Nadav 1 [2][4]	1 Kgs 15.25
Asa 3 = Basha 1 [24]	1 Kgs 15.33
Asa 26 = Ela 1 [2]	1 Kgs 16.8[5]

---

2. For discussion of these variants see also Begrich, *Chronologie*, pp. 58-63; Galil, *Chronology of the Kings of Israel and Judah*, pp. 155-62.

3. The Septuagint version of 1 Kgs 15.8-9 (Codex Vaticanus B) gives different figures for this synchronism. According to these verses Abiam died in Jeroboam's 24th regnal year and Asa became king in the same year. These variants disagree with the information given in 1 Kgs 14.20 that Jeroboam ruled for only 22 years.

4. In 1 Kgs 14.20 it is stated that Jeroboam reigned for 22 years. Synchronisms in 1 Kgs 15.9-10, 25 imply that Jeroboam reigned for only 21 years. Josephus (*Ant.* VIII.287) gives a synchronism Asa 3 = Nadav 1. It is also worth noting that according to 2 Chron. 13.20 Jeroboam I would have died already during the reign of Abiam. This statement should be related to the retribution theology of the Chronicler. The righteous Abiam who was attacked by Jeroboam saw the death of his wicked opponent.

2. The Chronological Data

Asa 27 = Zimri 1 [seven days]	1 Kgs 16.15
Asa 31 = Omri 1 [12][6]	1 Kgs 16.23
Asa 38 = Ahab 1 [22]	1 Kgs 16.29[7]
Jehoshaphat 1 [25] = Ahab 4	1 Kgs 22.41-42[8]
Jehoshaphat 17 = Ahaziah (Israel) 1 [2][9]	1 Kgs 22.52[10]
Jehoram (Judah) 2 = Jehoram (Israel) 1[11]	2 Kgs 1.17
Jehoshaphat 18 = Jehoram (Israel) 1 [12]	2 Kgs 3.1
Jehoram (Judah) 1 [8] = Jehoram (Israel) 5[12]	2 Kgs 8.16-17

5. The Septuagint (B) version states in 1 Kgs 16.6 that Elah became king in Asa's 20th regnal year. This would imply that Basha reigned for only 18 years – something which is in conflict with the information in 1 Kgs 15.33 – and is therefore hardly a reliable textual tradition. According to 2 Chron. 16.1 Basha would have attacked Judah in the 36th regnal year of Asa, which is apparently in conflict with the synchronism of 1 Kgs 16.8.

6. In the traditions behind the book of Kings there must be two different ways of calculating the beginning of the reign of Omri. If he reigned for twelve years and Ahab became king in Asa's 38th regnal year, then Omri must have become king already in Asa's 27th regnal year. This is a plausible assumption because after Zimri, Omri was elected as king by some Israelites while other selected Tibni as their king (1 Kgs 16.21). Therefore, we must assume that the period between Asa 27 and Asa 31 saw an internal-political struggle in Israel between Omri and Tibni. Only in Asa's 31st regnal year was Omri chosen as the king over the whole Israel (1 Kgs 16.22). This means that we do not have any tension in the synchronisms, only two different traditions calculating the beginning of the reign of Omri. Indeed, some Septuagint manuscripts read the year 27 instead of the year 31 here, but this is apparently a later corrective to the text.

7. According to the Septuagint (B) to 1 Kgs 16.29, Ahab would have become king in Jehoshaphat's 2nd regnal year. This synchronism has been calculated from the synchronism Jehoram (Judah) 1 = Jehoram (Israel) 5 in 2 Kgs 8.16-17 with an assumption that Ahab reigned for only 20 years.

8. The Septuagint (B) reads in 1 Kgs 16.28 that Jehoshaphat would have become king in Omri's 11th regnal year. This synchronism has probably been fabricated from 2 Kgs 1.17 according to which Jehoram (Judah) 2 = Jehoram (Israel) 1. We shall argue that this synchronism in 2 Kgs 1.17 cannot be correct, but is a result of later manipulation of chronological traditions. This implies that the synchronism given in the Septuagint B version of 1 Kgs 16.28 has been fabricated later.

9. Because Jehoshaphat became king in Ahab's 4th regnal year we receive Jehoshaphat 17 = Ahab 20 = Ahaziah 1 which implies that Ahab reigned for only 20 years and not for 22 years as stated in 1 Kgs 16.29.

10. Many of the Lucianic manuscripts of the Septuagint read here the synchronism Ahaziah (Israel) 1 = Jehoshaphat 24. This synchronism has been generated from Jehoram (Judah) 2 = Jehoram (Israel) 1 in 2 Kgs 1.17.

11. This synchronism is in tension with 2 Kgs 3.1 and 2 Kgs 8.16-17.

12. According to 1 Kgs 22.42, Jehoshaphat ruled for 25 years. This would give us a synchronism Jehoshaphat 25 = Jehoram (Judah) 1 = Jehoram (Israel) 8. It seems clear that we have some confusing traditions here.

Ahaziah (Judah) 1 [1] = Jehoram (Israel) 12	2 Kgs 8.25-26[13]
Ahaziah (Judah) 1 = Jehoram (Israel) 11	2 Kgs 9.29[14]
Athaliah [6/7]	2 Kgs 11.4
Joash 1 [40] = Jehu 7	2 Kgs 12.1
Joash 23 = Jehoahaz 1 [17]	2 Kgs 13.1
Joash 37 = Jehoash 1 [16]	2 Kgs 13.10[15]
Amaziah 1 [29] = Jehoash 2[16]	2 Kgs 14.1
Amaziah 15 = Jeroboam II 1 [41]	2 Kgs 14.23[17]
Uzziah 1 [52] = Jeroboam II 27[18]	2 Kgs 15.1[19]
Uzziah 38 = Zechariah 1 [6 months]	2 Kgs 15.8[20]
Uzziah 39 = Shallum 1 [1 month]	2 Kgs 15.13
Uzziah 39 = Menahem 1 [10]	2 Kgs 15.17
Uzziah 50 = Pekahiah 1 [2]	2 Kgs 15.23
Uzziah 52 = Pekah 1 [20]	2 Kgs 15.27
Jotham 1 [16] = Pekah 2	2 Kgs 15.32-33
Jotam 20 = Hosea 1[21]	2 Kgs 15.30

13. Some Septuagint manuscripts read the synchronism Ahaziah (Judah) 1 = Jehoram (Israel) 11 as in the MT version of 2 Kgs 9.29.

14. This synchronism is an interesting alternative to that in 2 Kgs 8.25-26, and indicates how ancient writers could use both alternatives for their calculations.

15. Some Septuagint manuscripts have the 39th regnal year of Joash here. This synchronism is in harmony with the synchronism in 2 Kgs 13.1 Joash 23 = Jehoahaz 1 when Jehoahaz reigned for 17 years. V. Pavlovsky and E. Vogt ('Die Jahre der Könige von Juda und Israel', *Biblica* 45 [1964], pp. 321-47, esp. 329) have argued that the Septuagint reading would be more original. However, they fail to see that there are several other cases in synchronisms where the difference of two years is presupposed. The MT reading is clearly *lectio difficilior*.

16. According to 2 Kgs 12.1-2 Joash reigned for 40 years. However this synchronism in 2 Kgs 14.1 together with 2 Kgs 13.10 implies that Joash would have reigned for only 38 years.

17. Josephus (*Ant*. IX.205) gives the synchronism Amaziah 11 = Jeroboam II 1.

18. This synchronism cannot be correct. The synchronism Amaziah 15 = Jeroboam II 1 in 2 Kgs 14.23 implies that Amaziah 29 = Uzziah 1 = Jeroboam II 15. In a similar way the synchronism Uzziah 38 = Zechariah 1 = Jeroboam II 41 in 2 Kgs 15.8 implies that Uzziah 1 = Jeroboam II 4.

19. Some Septuagint manuscript read here Uzziah 1 = Jeroboam II 15 – something which has been generated from the synchronism in 2 Kgs 14.23. Josephus (*Ant*. IX.216) gives Uzziah 1 = Jeroboam II 14.

20. Some Septuagint manuscripts read here Uzziah 28 = Zechariah 1, and others Uzziah 39 = Zechariah 1. These variations indicate the problems involved with the synchronism in 2 Kgs 15.1.

21. This is a curious synchronism because it refers to Jotham's 20th regnal year even though he reigned for only 16 years according to 2 Kgs 15.32-33. On the other hand, it corroborates quite well with the synchronism Jotham 1 = Pekah 2 because Pekah reigned for 20 years according to 2 Kgs 15.27 and after him Hosea became king. Therefore, we receive a synchronism Jotham 19 = Pekah 20, and Hosea 1 could well correspond to Jotham 20 in that case.

Ahaz 1 [16] = Pekah 17	2 Kgs 16.1-2
Ahaz 12 = Hosea 1 [9][22]	2 Kgs 17.1[23]
Hezekiah 1 [29] = Hosea 3[24]	2 Kgs 18.1-2
Hezekiah 4 = Hosea 7 = Samaria's besiege begins	2 Kgs 18.9
Hezekiah 6 = Hosea 9 = Samaria's fall	2 Kgs 17.6; 18.10-11
Hezekiah 14 = Sennacherib's invasion in Judah	2 Kgs 18.13

The chronological data of the books of Kings are formally reminiscent of those in the Babylonian Chronicle. In this extra-biblical document we have synchronisms between the Babylonian kings and their neighboring kings as well as the Babylonian kings and important political events.[25] This indicates that we have good reason to date the chronological system which is followed in the books of Kings to the pre-exilic time assuming that redaction-critical arguments support such a date.

As mentioned in the footnotes, there are some internal tensions between these synchronisms which imply that the biblical chronological system is inconsistent, and moreover, that this is not dependent on the way we evaluate it with the aid of the extra-biblical documents. In particular, there are three periods where synchronisms of the Israelite and Judean kings are confusing. The *first* period is the end of the dynasty of Omri and the beginning of the dynasty of Jehu in Israel and the reign of Athaliah in Judah. This is well illustrated by 2 Kgs 1.17 and 2 Kgs 3.1 which give two different dates to the accession of Jehoram, the king of Israel. The *second* problem is the synchronism Uzziah 1 = Jeroboam II 27 (2 Kgs 15.1) which stands in apparent conflict with the preceding and following synchronisms, and seems to be an isolated and erroneous tradition in the books of Kings. *Finally*, we have confusing synchronisms during the time of the Syro-Ephraimite war which is well illustrated with

---

22. According to 2 Kgs 15.27 Pekah reigned for 20 years which together with 2 Kgs 16.1-2 imply that we should receive a synchronism Ahaz 4 = Pekah 20 = Hosea 1. This is in tension with the information given in 2 Kgs 17.1.

23. Some Septuagint manuscripts read here the synchronism Ahaz 10 = Hosea 1.

24. According to 2 Kgs 16.1-2 Ahaz reigned for 16 years. Assuming that the synchronism Ahaz 12 = Hosea 1 [9] in 2 Kgs 17.1 is correct, we should receive Ahaz 16 = Hezekiah 1 = Hosea 5 – something which is in tension with the synchronism given in 2 Kgs 18.1-2. On the other hand, if we assume that Ahaz reigned for 16 years and calculate from the synchronism Ahaz 1 [16] = Pekah 17 in 2 Kgs 16.1-2 we received Ahaz 4 = Hosea 1 and consequently Ahaz 12 = Hosea 9 and thus Hezekiah would have become king of Judah only 4 years after the destruction of Samaria (= Hosea 9).

25. For this see J. Lewy, *Die Chronologie der Könige von Israel und Juda* (Giessen: Alfred Töpelmann, 1927); A.K. Grayson, *Assyrian and Babylonian Chronicles* (Texts from Cuneiform Sources; Locust Valley: J.J. Augustin, 1975), pp. 1-67.

the reign of Pekah and synchronisms like Ahaz 1 = Pekah 17 in 2 Kgs 16.1-2 and Ahaz 12 = Hosea 1 in 2 Kgs 17.1 as well as Hezekiah 1 = Hosea 3 in 2 Kgs 18.1-2.

Before we scrutinize this biblical system of regnal years of the Israelite and Judean kings we shall first look what kind of additional challenges extra-biblical documents give to it.

The Challenge of Extra-biblical Documents to the Biblical Chronological System

There are many important historical documents which make it possible to fix ancient Near Eastern chronology to our modern chronology. The following documents can be mentioned:

Assyrian eponym lists can be fixed to the absolute chronology because they mention the solar eclipse in Ashur-Dan III's reign which took place in 15 June 763 BCE.[26] In addition, these eponym lists can be put in exact harmony with the reigns of the Assyrian kings under the period of 910-612 BCE.[27] These absolute dates give us a chronological framework against which several biblical events can be fixed as, for example, the so-called Syro-Ephraimite war (2 Kgs 15.29; 16.1-9; Isa. 7.1-17), the destruction of Samaria (2 Kgs 17.1-6; 18.9-11), Sargon II's attack against Ashdod (Isa. 20) and Sennacherib's invasion in Judah (2 Kgs 18.13-19.38; Isa. 36–37).

The Babylonian Chronicle completes historical and chronological details in Assyrian documents.[28] It gives us detailed chronological information about the Neo-Babylonian period and is an important source for the dating of the destruction of Jerusalem (2 Kgs 25) and events preceding it including, for example, the death of Josiah (when Necho came to assist Assyria in Harran; 2 Kgs 23.29-30), the battle of Carchemish (where Nebuchadnezzar defeated the Egyptian army and took control over Palestine; Jer. 46.2) and the first conquest of Jerusalem in the reign of Jeconiah (2 Kgs 24.8-17).[29]

---

26. 'In Siwan the sun had an eclipse'. For this see A. Millard, *The Eponyms of the Assyrian Empire 910–612 BC* (SAAS, 2; Helsinki: The Neo-Assyrian Text Corpus Project, 1994), pp. 41, 58.

27. For this see Millard, *Eponyms of the Assyrian Empire*, p. 13.

28. See D.J. Wiseman, *Chronicles of Chaldean Kings (626–556 B.C.) in the British Museum* (London: The Trustees of the British Museum, 1956); Grayson, *Assyrian and Babylonian Chronicles*.

29. Parker and Dubberstein (*Babylonian Chronology*) have fixed the reigns of the Babylonian kings to the absolute chronology during the period 626 BCE–75 CE.

Another important document from the later period is the Milesian eponymous list of *aisymnetai* – also called *stephanephoroi* – which continues with lacunae to the reign of Tiberius. The document contains a complete list of eponymous posts from 525/24 BCE until Alexander the Great in 334/33 BCE.[30] This being the case we have a chronological line during the period 525–333 BCE which enables us to fix the timeline between Alexander the Great and the Persian Empire.[31] In addition to these two eponym lists we have several important Assyrian, Babylonian, Persian and Greek documents which also give us the possibility to fix the chronological events of the ancient Near East quite securely from the neo-Assyrian period in 10th and 9th centuries BCE to the destruction of the Second Temple in 70 CE.[32]

Extra-biblical documents challenge the biblical chronology because they fix some events mentioned in the Bible to the absolute chronology. Because these events are also connected to certain regnal years of the Israelite and Judean kings, this enables us to evaluate the reliability of the biblical chronology.

According to the biblical chronology, the destruction of Samaria took place in Hosea's 9th regnal year which is synchronized with Hezekiah's 6th regnal year (2 Kgs 17.4-6; 18.9-11). According to the Babylonian Chronicle, the besieging of Samaria began in the reign of Shalmaneser V (727–722 BCE) when the Assyrian king 'ravaged Samaria' before he died.[33] After the death of Shalmaneser V Sargon II apparently had to secure his throne in Assyria, and only in his second regnal year i.e. 720 BCE did he return to the West and is reported as having deported 27,290 inhabitants of Samaria. What remains obscure here is whether the city was destroyed during the reign of Shalmaneser V as noted in the Babylonian Chronicle, or only in the reign of Sargon II. In any case 2 Kgs 17.5-6 has telescoped the events in 722–720 BCE. The city was taken by Shalmaneser V in 722 but perhaps not yet then destroyed, and at least the people of Samaria had not yet been deported. Later Sargon II concluded the fate of Samaria by (destroying it and) deporting its inhabitants to Assyria.[34]

---

30. E.J. Bickerman, *Chronology of the Ancient World* (London: Thames & Hudson, rev. edn, 1980).

31. It is worth noting that Dan. 11.2-4 speaks of only four Persian kings before Alexander the Great. See further Chapter 5.

32. For this see Bickerman, *Chronology*; J. Finegan, *The Handbook of Biblical Chronology*, pp. 245-69.

33. Grayson, *Assyrian and Babylonian Chronicles*, p. 73.

34. For this see M. Cogan and H. Tadmor, *II Kings* (AB, 11; New York: Doubleday & Co., 1988), pp. 195-202.

Another important fixed point is the invasion of Sennacherib to Judah in 701 BCE. According to the biblical chronology this took place in Hezekiah's 14th regnal year. This being the case there were about 20 years between the destruction of Samaria (722–720 BCE) and the invasion of Sennacherib to Judah (702/01 BCE), and these cannot be placed between Hezekiah's 6th and his 14th regnal year.

The date of Sennacherib's invasion of Judah in Hezekiah's 14th regnal year (702/01 BCE) indicates another chronological problem. We know that Jerusalem was destroyed in Zedekiah's 11th regnal year and the event must be dated to 587 or 586 BCE.[35] Within the 115 year timeframe, we cannot fit Hezekiah's last 15 years together with the regnal periods of Manasseh (55 years), Ammon (2 years), Josiah (31 years), Shallum (3 months), Jehoiakim (11 years), Jeconiah (3 months) and Zedekiah (11 years), as together these total about 125 years.

Assyrian documents indicate that Menahem paid tribute to Tiglat-Pileser III in 738 BCE.[36] Between this event and the destruction of Samaria (722–20 BCE) there were about 17 years. But the lengths of the reigns of the Israelite kings after Menahem consist of Pekahiah (2 years), Pekah (20 years) and Hosea (9 years) which together are about 31 years and exceed the 17 year timeframe. Pekah was dethroned as the result of the Syro-Ephraimite war (734–732 BCE), and it is impossible to fit his twenty-year reign in between 738 BCE and 732 BCE.[37] On the other hand, the nine-year reign of Hosea fits quite nicely in between 731 BCE and 722 BCE.

Further, the Assyrian chronological system implies that Jehu paid tribute to Shalmaneser III in 841 BCE.[38] Between this event and the destruction and deportation of Samaria (722–720 BCE) there are about 120 years. After Jehu the following kings reigned in Israel according to

35. Concerning different scholarly opinions on when Jerusalem was destroyed see C. Shedl, 'Nochmals das Jahr der Zerströrung Jerusalems: 587 oder 586 v. Chr.', *ZAW* 74 (1962), pp. 209-13; H. Cazelles, '587 ou 586?', in C.L. Meyers and M. O'Connor (eds.), *The Word of the Lord Shall Go Forth* (Winona Lake: Eisenbrauns, 1983), pp. 427-35; E. Kutsch, 'Das Jahr des Katastrophe: 587 v. Chr.', *Biblica* 55 (1974), pp. 520-45; Hayes and Hooker, *New Chronology*, pp. 95-98; Galil, *The Chronology of the Kings of Israel and Judah*, pp. 108-26. We shall return to this problem in Chapter 4.

36. H. Tadmor, *The Inscriptions of Tiglath-Pileser III King of Assyria* (Jerusalem: The Israel Academy of Sciences and Humanities, 1994), pp. 66-69, 106-107, 274-76.

37. Tadmor, *Inscriptions of Tiglath-Pileser III*, pp. 140-41, 170-71, 188-89, 202-203, 277.

38. A.K. Grayson, *Assyrian Rulers of the Early First Millennium BC II (858–745 BC)* (RIMA, 3; Toronto: University of Toronto Press, 1996).

2 Kings: Jehoahaz 17, Joash 16, Jeroboam 41, Menahem 10, Pekahiah 2, Pekah 20, Hosea 9 = 115 years. These regnal years could fit between 841 BCE and 722–21 BCE. However, we must consider the fact that the Israelite king Ahab battled against Shalmaneser III at Qarqar in 853 BCE only 12 years before Jehu paid tribute in 841 BCE. After Ahab, Ahaziah reigned for 2 years and after him Jehoram for 12 years. From these chronological data it becomes clear that Jehu must have paid his tribute at the beginning of his reign. As Jehu reigned for 28 years, the lengths of the reigns of the Israelite kings from Jehu to the destruction of Samaria do not fit between the years 841 BCE and 722–21 BCE. And further we may ask whether the reigns of Ahaziah and Jehoram can be dated between 853 BCE and 841 BCE?

This being the case we disagree with Thiele who emphasizes that the biblical chronology is accurate between Jehu's paying of tribute and the destruction of Samaria.[39]

---

39. See Thiele's view in 'Coregencies', pp. 198-99, discussed above in Chapter 1.

3

RELIABILITY OF THE SYNCHRONIC TRADITION OF THE ISRAELITE AND JUDEAN KINGS

Do We Have a Reliable Tradition for the Biblical Chronology on the Reigns of Kings?

In the beginning of Chapter 2 we have seen that there are, in particular, three periods where synchronisms of the Israelite and Judean kings are in conflict with each other: (1) The end of the dynasty of Omri; (2) The accession year of Uzziah; and (3) The Israelite and Judean synchronisms around the reign of Pekah and the destruction of Samaria. Extra-biblical documents confirm that the biblical chronology around the reign of Pekah is problematic. It is clear that Pekah cannot have been king in Israel for 20 years. We have also seen that extra-biblical documents make it difficult to fit the reigns of Jehoram (12 years) and Ahaziah (2 years) between the battle of Qarqar in 853 BCE, when Ahab was king in Israel, and the tribute of Jehu in 841 BCE. This being the case, extra-biblical documents confirm what we know already from biblical synchronisms: the chronological system during the time of Pekah and around the end of the dynasty of Omri and the beginning of the dynasty of Jehu is problematic.

We shall now discuss whether it is possible to explain how these problematic synchronisms have been generated. We shall do this *purely by arguing with biblical synchronisms without any reference to extra-biblical documents or any attempts to relate the reigns to the absolute chronology*. While scholars often try to solve these problematic synchronisms by assuming co-regency we shall avoid such explanations if there is no clear biblical reference to such a possibility.

3. *Reliability of the Synchronic Tradition*

The Case of Uzziah 1 = Jeroboam II 27

The best way to begin is the synchronism Uzziah 1 = Jeroboam II 27 in 2 Kgs 15.1 which cannot be correct.[1] There is an attempt to explain the outcome of this synchronism by referring to co-regency.[2] However, we shall not begin our attempt to understand this problematic synchronism by such a hypothetical assumption before we have taken other relevant arguments into account.

If we start to calculate from the synchronism Uzziah 50 = Pekahiah 1 in 2 Kgs 15.23 we receive Uzziah 50 (or Uzziah 49) = Menahem 10 and consequently Uzziah 41 (or Uzziah 40) = Menahem 1 = Jeroboam II 41, and in that case we receive a synchronism Uzziah 1 = Jeroboam II 1 or Uzziah 1 = Jeroboam II 2. In a similar way the synchronism Uzziah 38 = Zechariah 1 in 2 Kgs 15.8 gives us Uzziah 38 (or Uzziah 37) = Jeroboam II 41, and we receive Uzziah 1 = Jeroboam II 4 or Uzziah 1 = Jeroboam II 5. This being the case, the synchronisms in the later reign of Uzziah imply that Uzziah and Jeroboam II became kings at about the same time in Israel and in Judah respectively. Such a view is clearly in tension with the synchronism Uzziah 1 = Jeroboam II 27 in 2 Kgs 15.1. How can we explain the outcome of the synchronism in 2 Kgs 15.1? I would like to suggest the following explanation.

2 Kings 14.17 contains an interesting detail that 'Amaziah son of Joash (יוֹאָשׁ) king of Judah lived for fifteen years after the death of Jehoash (יְהוֹאָשׁ) son of Jehoahaz king of Israel'. Such information is an unusual chronological detail in the Books of Kings and we can ask whether originally its aim was to assert that Amaziah lived for fifteen years after the death of his father Joash. That would mean that this tradition about the death of Joash was misunderstood as referring to the death of Jehoash and the result was a lengthening of the reign of Amaziah from 15 years to 29 years.[3] If this is so then we can conclude that Uzziah became king soon after Amaziah 15 and it is possible to

---

1. Galil (*Chronology of the Kings of Israel and Judah*, p. 60 n. 47) lists several reasons why this synchronism cannot be correct. Nevertheless, he presents on pp. 60-61 quite an artificial solution of many subsequent coregencies in Judah. As noted in Chapter 1 (Introduction) we should be careful not to refer to this *deus ex machina* explanation.

2. Thiele, *Mysterious Numbers*, pp. 69-71; Hayes and Hooker, *New Chronology*, p. 54.

3. Thiele (*Mysterious Numbers*, pp. 68-71; *A Chronology of the Hebrew Kings*, pp. 39-45), Hayes and Hooker (*New Chronology*, pp. 41-52) and Galil (*Chronology of the Kings of Israel and Judah*, pp. 57-59) argue for the coregency of Uzziah with Amaziah. In my judgment, such an assumption is unwarranted.

suggest the synchronism Uzziah 1 = Jeroboam II 2 – and this proposal is in harmony with the above synchronism derived from the synchronism of Uzziah 50 = Pekahiah 1 (2 Kgs 15.23).

The lengthening of the reign of Amaziah by 15 years led to the change of the beginning of the reign of Uzziah from Jeroboam II 2 to Jeroboam II 17. The outcome of the synchronism in 2 Kgs 15.1 can finally be explained in such a way that at an early stage the Hebrew 17 has been read erroneously as 27 – something which is possible.

In this case the synchronisms in 2 Kings 13–15 give us two different chronological frameworks which slightly differ from each other. I have italicised all synchronisms which can be found in 2 Kings 13–15:

Tradition A:

Judah	Israel
Joash 1	= Jehu 8
Joash 21	= Jehu 28 = Jehoahaz 1
Joash 37	= Jehoahaz 17 = *Jehoash 1*
Joash 40 = Amaziah 1	= Jehoash 4
Amaziah 13	= Jeroboam II 1
Amaziah 15	= Jeroboam II 3
Uzziah 1	= Jeroboam II 4
Uzziah 38	= *Jeroboam 41 = Zechariah 1*
Uzziah 39	= *Shallum 1 = Menahem 1*
Uzziah 48	= Menahem 10 = Pekahiah 1

Tradition B:

Judah	Israel
Joash 1	= Jehu 6
Joash 23	= Jehu 28 = *Jehoahaz 1*
Joash 39	= Jehoahaz 17 = Jehoash 1
Joash 40 = Amaziah 1	= *Jehoash 2*
Amaziah 15	= *Jeroboam II 1*
Uzziah 1	= Jeroboam II 2
Uzziah 40	= Jeroboam 41 = Zechariah 1
Uzziah 41	= Shallum 1 = Menahem 1
Uzziah 50	= Menahem 10 = Pekahiah 1

These constructed hypothetical traditions differ by two years, and we can see that the synchronisms of Tradition A agree with those in the Deuteronomistic History when the accession years of some Israelite kings are referred to, while the synchronisms in Tradition B correspond to those in the Deuteronomistic History when the accession years of the Judean kings and the accession years of Jeroboam II and Jehoahaz are referred to. This two year difference implies that it is impossible to put the synchronisms in harmony with the aid of accession-year and non-accession-year systems. Additionally, we have seen that we have other reasonable arguments to explain some conflicting synchronisms than the presupposition that co-regency had taken place. In particular, we have argued that in an early chronological tradition the synchronism Uzziah 1 = Jeroboam II 2 existed – as is implied from synchronisms in 2 Kgs 15.8, 23. From that synchronism the new synchronism Uzziah 1 = Jeroboam II 17 was fabricated, and which in turn during the transmission process of the biblical text was miscopied to Uzziah 1 = Jeroboam II 27.

The disagreement between these two conflicting traditions seems to go back to the revolt of Jehu. The tumultuous years of Jehu's revolution led to the reign of Athaliah which lasted for six years, and which was seen to correspond to Jehu's regnal years 1–6. This resulted in the synchronism Joash 1 = Jehu 7 (2 Kgs 12.1). The Deuteronomist who knew both the Traditions A and B, varied between synchronisms in them when he presented the history of Israel and Judah. If this is the case then we could reconstruct the following transmission process of these synchronisms:

1. The Deuteronomist who wrote his version of history during the exile knew two different traditions where synchronisms differed by two years from each other. He used them both and did not aim to present an ironclad chronological system. Rather, he wanted to present the history of Israel and Judah as he knew it from tradition, by emphasizing his own important theological tendencies. On the one hand the Deuteronomist was a historian who transmitted older traditions, on the other hand he was a theologian who attempted to understand the catastrophe of the exile. Synchronisms belong clearly to the 'basket' of history.
2. These two traditions were constructed earlier by pre-Deuteronomistic authors who were interested in presenting the history of Israel and Judah in conjunction with each other. These authors may have received some synchronisms from royal archives, but in the main they reconstructed their own versions of synchronic chronology from the length of the reigns of the Israelite and Judean kings. Consequently, they differ slightly from each other.
3. It is impossible to say when exactly Traditions A and B were composed, nonetheless it is reasonable to assume that they were made during the time when the kingdom of Judah still existed but the kingdom of Israel had been destroyed. Such a date is not

in tension with the fact that the synchronic chronological system transmitted in the Books of Kings is reminiscent of the Mesopotamian tradition (the Babylonian Chronicle).[4]

4. It seems clear that these two different traditions are based on the same sources in royal archives which, however, have been interpreted in two different ways, in two different directions so that synchronisms differ from each other by two years.

The Case of Omri's Dynasty

We have seen that the chronological system is quite consistent from the time after Solomon onwards, but that there are apparent problems at the end of Omri's dynasty.[5] First of all we have three conflicting synchronisms in 2 Kgs 1.17 (Jehoram/Judah 2 = Jehoram/Israel 1), 2 Kgs 3.1 (Jehoshaphat 18 = Jehoram/Israel 1) and 2 Kgs 8.16-17 (Jehoram/Judah 1 = Jehoram/Israel 5). The best proposal for the outcome of these conflicting synchronisms is (if it can be explained) that one of them is a reliable tradition which has been used to fabricate the other erroneous synchronisms.

Hayes and Hooker have attempted to solve the problem in such a way that Jehoram of Judah and Jehoram of Israel were one and the same person, the son of Jehoshaphat, the king of Judah.[6] This proposal goes back to Strange's article where he argues that Jehoram of Israel is, in fact, the 'ghost-Joram' and the same-named king of Israel appears only in the Deuteronomistic framework.[7] The proposal of 'ghost-Jehoram' in

4. Concerning the theory that there once was a synchronic chronicle from David to the fall of Samaria see A. Jepsen, *Die Quellen des Königsbuches* (Halle: Niemeyer, 1953), pp. 30-40. See also H. Weippert, 'Die "deuteronomistischen" Beurteilungen der Könige von Israel und Juda und das Problem der Redaktion der Königsbücher', *Biblica* 53 (1972), pp. 301-39. See further good surveys presented in H. Weippert, 'Das deuteronomistische Geshichtswerk: sein Ziel und Ende in der neueren Forschung', *Theologische Rundschau* NF 50 (1985), pp. 213-49; B. Halpern and A. Lemaire, 'The Composition of Kings', in Lemaire and Halpern (eds.), *The Books of Kings*, pp. 123-53. It is clear from these surveys that a synchronic tradition dating from about the time of the destruction of Samaria is a plausible option.

5. Galil (*Chronology of the Kings of Israel and Judah*, p. 12) notes that Jeroboam I and Rehoboam began to rule at the same time and Jehoram of Israel and Ahaziah of Judah were both killed in the revolt of Jehu, but the regnal years from Jeroboam I to Jehoram are 98 while from Rehoboam to Ahaziah only 95.

6. Hayes and Hooker, *New Chronology*, pp. 32-36.

7. J. Strange, 'Joram, King of Israel and Judah', *VT* 25 (1975), pp. 191-201. In fact, Strange notes that this idea of one Jehoram appears already in S.A. Cook's remark in *Cambridge Ancient History*.

Israel was put forward before the finding of the Aramaic Tel Dan Inscription, in which it is possible to read fragmentarily how the Israel-Judah-coalition was defeated, presumably by the king of Aram:[8]

7' [And I killed...]ram son of [...]
8'. the king of Israel, and I killed [...]yahu son of [...the ki]/ng of
9'. the House of David.

The option of completing the text so that reference is made to Jehoram, the king of Israel and Ahaziyahu, the king of Judah (= the House of David), is a plausible one.[9] Indeed, 2 Kgs 9.14-28 supports such an interpretation. The text refers to the battle where Hazael, the king of Aram, managed to wound Jehoram. As a consequence Jehu organised a rebellion and killed Jehoram as well as Ahaziah, the king of Judah. It seems that the Aramaic inscription interpreted the events so that Jehoram was wounded in the battle and because he died later, the Aramean king could boast that he had killed him.[10] The troops from Judah probably assisted Israel in that battle – something which can easily be related to the biblical account because Ahaziah visited Jezreel to meet Jehoram. This being the case the Tel Dan Inscription gives clear evidence to the conclusion that Israel had a king whose name was Jehoram at the same time as Judah had a king named Ahaziah.

It is worth noting that during the reigns of Jehoram and Ahaziah in Judah there were close contacts between Judah and Israel. One indication for these political ties was the marriage between Jehoram of Judah and Athaliah of Israel. 2 Kings 8.18 (and its parallel verse 2 Chron. 21.6)

---

8. See the inscription in A. Biran and J. Naveh, 'An Aramaic Stele Fragment from Tel Dan', *IEJ* 43 (1993), pp. 81-93; Biran and Naveh, 'The Tel Dan Inscription: A New Fragment', *IEJ* 45 (1995), pp. 1-18; and its interpretation in W.M. Schniedewind, 'Tel Dan Stela: New Light on Aramaic and Jehu's Revolt', *BASOR* 302 (1996), pp. 75-90. For another view of the way the two fragments should be combined see G. Athas, *The Tel Dan Inscription: A Reappraisal and a New Interpretation* (London: T. & T. Clark 2003); Athas, 'Setting the Record Straight: What Are We Making of the Tel Dan Inscription?', *JSS* 51 (2006), pp. 241-55.

9. It was common custom to call the kingdom according to the founder of the dynasty as, for example, the Assyrian sources use the name 'the House of Omri' for the Kingdom of Israel. For this see G. Rendsburg, 'On the Writing of *bytdwd* in the Aramaic Inscription of Tel Dan', *IEJ* 45 (1995), pp. 22-25.

10. See the similar case which is detected in Shalmaneser III's inscriptions, where the Monolith Inscription states that the inhabitants of the region of Balih killed their lord Giammu who had opposed Shalmaneser but then in the later text of Shalmaneser's annals this detail has been formulated so that the Assyrian king himself killed Giammu. For this see Schniedewind, 'Tel Dan Stela', esp. p. 84.

states that Athaliah was the daughter of Ahab.[11] This marriage took place before Jehoram became king in Judah and implies close political cooperation between Jehoshaphat and Ahab – something which is indicated in 1 Kings 22. This being the case the double attestation of the names Jehoram and Ahaziah in Israel and Judah could be explained simply as their being proofs of close family ties. That they also cause problem for later editors and, in particular, for synchronisms is indicated in biblical evidence as we have seen.[12]

In order to solve this enigma of the reigns of two Jehorams and two Ahaziahs the best starting-point is to argue that one of the biblical synchronisms is based on reliable annalistic sources and the other synchronisms are simply later fabrications. 2 Kings 1.17 implies that Jehoram/Judah was already king when Jehoram/Israel became king, while 2 Kgs 8.16-17 states that Jehoram/Judah became king when Jehoram/Israel began to reign. If we assume that synchronism in 2 Kgs 8.16-17 (Jehoram/Judah 1 = Jehoram/Israel 5) is right we should find an explanation model for the outcome of the synchronism in 2 Kgs 1.17. A plausible explanation for the outcome of the erroneous synchronisms could be the fact that both kings with the name Ahaziah reigned a very short time (two years and one year). This may have led to the confusion between the years of death of the kings Ahaziah of Israel and Ahaziah of Judah. Another presupposition is that the length of the reigns of Jehoram (Israel) and Jehoram (Judah) are incorrect and have been lengthened in the transmission process. In that case we must establish the length of the reign of Jehoram (Judah) so that the outcome of the other synchronism can be explained. It seems that in that case the right length of the reign of Jehoram (Judah) must be two years. Thus we receive the following list of synchronisms:[13]

---

11. 2 Kgs 8.26 (and its parallel passage 2 Chron. 22.2) states that Athaliah was the daughter of Omri. However, the Hebrew word *bat* can also be understood as granddaughter.

12. Strange ('Joram, King of Israel and Judah', pp. 196-97) also discusses 2 Chron. 21.4 and argues that the information of this verse originates from (reliable) annalistic sources and indicates that Jehoram of Judah killed Israelite officials (or princes). The question is whether we can regard 2 Chron. 21.4 as originating from early reliable royal archives. For this, see especially H.G.M. Williamson, *1 and Chronicles* (Grand Rapids: Eerdmans, 1982), pp. 247-48, 304. Of course, we can always present a possible world where the political circumstances led to the presence of Israel's officials in Jerusalem. There may have been some doubts about this conspiracy which would have led to the elimination of Judean and Israelite elites.

13. Cf. Begrich, *Chronologie*, pp. 106-10; Jepsen, 'Zur Chronologie', pp. 39-42.

3. Reliability of the Synchronic Tradition

Israel		Judah
Ahaziah 1		
Ahaziah 2	Jehoram 1	
	Jehoram 5	= Jehoram 1
	Jehoram 6	= Jehoram 2 = Ahaziah 1
	Jehoram 7 = Jehu 1	= Athaliah 1

From these figures we can explain the outcome of all other erroneous synchronisms in 2 Kgs 1.17; 3.1; 8.25-26. It was known that Ahaziah (Judah) died in the same year as Jehoram (Judah) because his reign was brief, not more than a year. Therefore the synchronism Ahaziah (Judah) 1 = Jehoram (Judah) 2 was established. This Ahaziah of Judah could then have been erroneously related to the king of Israel and because Jehoram/Israel became king after him we receive the synchronism Jehoram/Israel 1 = Jehoram/Judah 2 in 2 Kgs 1.17. This synchronism lived in its own life in pre-Deuteronomistic traditions and led to the lengthening of the reign of Jehoram/Judah because the reigns of Jehu and Athaliah begun at the same time. Thus we receive the following synchronisms:

Israel	Judah
Jehoram 1	= Jehoram 2
Jehoram 6	= Jehoram 7
Jehoram 7	= Jehoram 8 = Ahaziah 1
Jehu 1	= Athaliah 1

The reign of Jehoram/Judah was lengthened to 8 years (as stated in 2 Kgs 8.16-17). But this lengthening of the reign of Jehoram/Judah in turn led to the lengthening of the reign of Jehoram/Israel when the reliable synchronism Jehoram/Israel 5 = Jehoram/Judah 1 was taken as the starting-point for the calculations in another tradition. Thus we receive the following table:

Israel	Judah
Jehoram 5	= Jehoram 1
Jehoram 11	= Jehoram 7
Jehoram 12	= Jehoram 8 = Ahaziah 1
Jehu 1	= Athaliah 1

In this way we can explain the erroneous synchronism Ahaziah/Judah 1 = Jehoram/Israel 12 [11] (2 Kgs 8.25-26 [2 Kgs 9.29]). It seems clear that the Deuteronomist himself cannot be responsible for these three conflicting synchronisms. Neither can we assume that he lengthened the reigns of Jehoram. It seems quite obvious that he received these conflicting synchronisms with the lengthening of the reigns from tradition. Indeed, we can see that these conflicting synchronisms are related to different tradition blocks: 2 Kgs 1.17-18 is closely connected with the Elijah story and the synchronism could well have been fabricated by the pre-Deuteronomistic transmitter of the story. The synchronism in 2 Kgs 3.1 opens with the story of Moab's revolt against Israel and the Deuteronomist probably received it in this context. The synchronism in 2 Kgs 8.16 has an interesting formulation: 'In the fifth year of Joram son of Ahab king of Israel, when Jehoshaphat (still) was king of Judah, Jehoram son of Jehoshaphat began his reign as king of Judah'. This statement can be understood in such a way that the Deuteronomist received in tradition a synchronism Jehoram/Israel 5 = Jehoram/Judah 1 but realized that according to the synchronism in 2 Kgs 3.1 Jehoshaphat should still have been reigning in Judah. This being the case we may take the phrase 'when Jehoshaphat (still) was king of Judah' as a Deuteronomistic remark. Alternatively we can assume that a later copyist noticed this tension and added this phrase as a remark in the marginal.[14] In any case there is no need to presuppose any co-regency here. 2 Kings 8.25-26; 9.29 are synchronisms which relate the enthronement of Ahaziah the king of Judah to the reign of Jehoram (Israel). The synchronism in 2 Kgs 8.25-26 can be regarded as originating from a pre-Deuteronomistic tradition which is not directly based on the royal archive because it contains an inaccuracy in stating that Athaliah had been the daughter of Omri. 2 Kings 9.29 in turn is clearly an editorial comment to the story of Ahaziah and is based on the developed tradition in 2 Kgs 8.25-26.

This explanation gives us the possibility of putting the synchronisms of the earlier kings of Judah and Israel in quite good correspondence with each other. As already noted there are some problems because Ahab's regnal years are said to be 22 (as stated in 1 Kgs 16.29) or only 20 years depending on the synchronisms in 1 Kgs 22.52 and 2 Kgs 3.1. However,

---

14. This being the case there is no need to use the verse as an indication that co-regency had taken place in Judah – an idea which is presented by Thiele (*The Mysterious Numbers of the Hebrew Kings* 65). Galil (*Chronology of the Kings of Israel and Judah*, pp. 39-41) has two interesting observations. On p. 40 he writes that 'the words 'Jehoshaphat being then king of Judah' apparently do not constitute proof of the coronation of Jehoram in the lifetime of his father'. However, on the following p. 41 he writes: 'Jehoram was installed probably in 851, during the lifetime of his father Jehoshaphat'. It is difficult to reconcile these two statements. Hughes (*Secrets of Times*, pp. 105-106) explains the phrase 'while Jehoshaphat was king of Judah' as dittography, because it is not attested in most Septuagint manuscripts and can be explained as originating from an almost similar phrase in the same verse. See further Jepsen, 'Zur Chronologie', pp. 39-42.

because we have seen that the synchronism in 2 Kgs 3.1 is a later fabrication there is reason to accept 22 years as the right length for the reign of Ahab. The following list illustrates our possible harmonization of the synchronisms:

Israel	Judah
Jeroboam 18	Abiam 1
Jeroboam 20	Abiam 3 = Asa 1
Jeroboam 21 = Nadav 1	Asa 2
Nadav 2 = Baasha 1	Asa 3
Basha 24 = Elah 1	Asa 26
Elah 2 = Zimri = Omri 1	Asa 27
Omri 5 (sole regent in Israel)	Asa 31
Omri 12 = Ahab 1	Asa 38
Ahab 4	Asa 41 = Jehoshaphat 1
Ahab 22 = Ahaziah 1	Jehoshaphat 19
Ahaziah 2	Jehoshaphat 20
Jehoram 1	Jehoshaphat 21
Jehoram 4	Jehoshaphat 24
Jehoram 5	Jehoram 1
Jehoram 6	Jehoram 2 = Ahaziah 1
Jehoram 7 = Jehu 1	Athaliah 1

This explanation is not in exact harmony with the biblical synchronisms during the reigns of Ahab and Jehoshaphat; however, there are only differences by one or two years – something which corresponds well to our results from the time of Jehu and Athaliah to the time of Menahem and Uzziah.

Summing up we can conclude that many of the synchronisms between Rehoboam // Jeroboam I and Athaliah // Jehu transmitted in the Deuteronomistic History are based on pre-Deuteronomistic traditions.

The Case of Pekah

The third apparent problem pertaining to the biblical chronological system is the fact that according to the Assyrian records Menahem paid tribute to Tiglat-Pileser III during the Assyrian invasion of Palestine in 738 BCE or immediately after that invasion. On the other hand, the Assyrian documents also reveal that Pekah was dethroned as the consequence of the Syro-Ephraimite War in 734–732 BCE. This being the case it is an absolute impossibility that Pekah would have been king in Israel for 20 years. The chronological frames give us an indication that Pekah could have reigned for only 4 years, not more.[15] But this chronological problem caused by the Assyrian documents is not the only problem we have. We have already noted that even biblical synchronisms are in tensions with each other in 2 Kings 15–18. Therefore, our task is to deal with the biblical synchronisms and ask if we can explain how conflicting synchronisms have been generated.

Na'aman has presented an attractive theory that Pekah sympathized with the dynasty of Jehu because he apparently came from Gilead and the biblical traditions indicate that Jehu too had close contacts with Gilead (see 2 Kgs 9.1-13) – something which is also true for Elijah and Elisha (1 Kgs 19.15-18; 2 Kgs 3.13-14).[16] Therefore, Pekah may have argued that the reigns of Shallum, Menahem and Pekahiah should be simply ignored and that he was the real follower of the dynasty of Jehu.[17] The problem with this solution is not only Menahem's and Pekahiah's reigns but also that Pekah's 20-year reign seems to fit well in the chronological system of 2 Kings. After all Pekah became king in Uzziah's 52th regnal year (2 Kgs 15.27) and Jotham ascended to the throne in Pekah's second regnal year (2 Kgs 15.32) and Ahaz in Pekah's 17th regnal year (2 Kgs 16.1). Therefore, I should like to propose another alternative to solve the outcome of Pekah's 20-year reign.

A good starting-point is 1 Chron. 5.17 which records that 'all these were entered in the genealogical records during the reigns of Jotham king of Judah and Jeroboam king of Israel'. The text refers to Jotham and Jerobeam II having been contemporaries. However, the synchronisms in 2 Kings do not accord with this statement because Jotham became king in Pekah's 2nd regnal year (2 Kgs 15.32-33). Therefore, it seems plausible to assume that behind 1 Chron. 5.17 is a tradition where Jotham's reigning period was contemporary with Jeroboam II's. According to 2 Kgs 15.5 Jotham ruled in Judah while his father became ill. 2 Kings 15.5 together with 1 Chron. 5.17 imply that Jotham had been coregent with his father before Uzziah 38 when Jeroboam II died and his son Zechariah became king (2 Kgs 15.8). In order to make Jotham and

---

15. In his short monograph (only seven pages) *Mesopotamian Guidelines for Biblical Chronology* (Monographic Journals of the Near East, Syro-Mesopotamian Studies, 4/1 May 1981), J. Reade suggests that Pekah should be eliminated from the Israelite king list. The name Pakaha in the annals of Tiglath-Pileser III de facto refers to Pekahiah.

16. The Elijah and Elisha cycles are often connected to pro-Jehu traditions which the Deuteronomist has then adopted and used for his own purposes. See, e.g., O.H. Steck, *Überlieferung und Zeitgeschichte in den Elia-Erzählungen* (WMANT, 26; Neukirchen–Vluyn: Neukirchener Verlag, 1968).

17. Na'aman, 'Kingdoms of Israel and Judah'.

Jeroboam II contemporaries requires that the first mentioned had been coregent with his father from at least Uzziah 37 onwards. This being the case we have the following synchronisms:

Uzziah 37 = Jotham 1
Uzziah 52 = Jotham 16

This reasoning indicates that the whole of Jotham's 16-year reigning period took place in the form of co-regency. On the other hand, we have the synchronism Uzziah 52 = Pekah 1 (2 Kgs 15.27). This synchronism indicates that the 16-year reign of Jotham overlaps with the last years of Uzziah. To suggest that Ahaz became king in Judah after Uzziah is thus a real possibility. The Deuteronomist argued that Jotham's 16-year reign should be placed after Uzziah and therefore had to lengthen the reign of Pekah from 4 years to 20 years. Therefore the Deuteronomist generated three wrong synchronisms from the right information Uzziah 52 = Pekah 1 in the following way:

Uzziah 52	*= Pekah 1*	*2 Kgs 15.27*
Jotham 1	= Pekah 2	2 Kgs 15.32-33
Jotham 16 = Ahaz 1	= Pekah 17	2 Kgs 16.1-2
Jotham 19	= Pekah 20	
Jotham 20	= Hosea 1	2 Kgs 15.30

This calculation could explain the erroneous synchronisms in 2 Kgs 15.32-33; 16.1-2. The synchronism Jotham 20 = Hosea 1 in 2 Kgs 15.30 implies that Hosea became king four years after the death of Uzziah.[18] In

---

18. It is worth noting that the synchronism Jotham 20 = Hosea 1 implies that Jotham ruled for 20 years instead of 16. This gives us the interesting opportunity to ask whether the figures 390 and 40 years in Ezek. 4 could be based on accurate chronological data known for the prophet in Jeconiah's fifth year of the exile. According to the Deuteronomistic chronological data, the lengths of the reigns from Solomon to Jeconiah were 422½ years in total, but if Jotham had ruled for 20 years instead of 16 then the figure would be 426½ years. Jeconiah's fifth year of the exile corresponds to Zedekiah's fourth regnal year, which give us the possibility to argue that Ezekiel calculated 430 years from the time of Solomon to his own time. If this is the case then Ezekiel's 390 years and 40 years, together 430 years, may be related to this period of time. However, the problem here is that Ezekiel 4 allocates Judah only 40 years, while giving Israel 390 years. On the other hand, in the book of Ezekiel the House of Israel denotes the cultic community of the Judean people which regards Jerusalem as the holy city. Therefore, 390 years may refer to the existence of the Judean kingdom, while 40 years is calculated for the tribe of Judah because Solomon represented that tribe. Another possibility is to regard 430 years as corresponding to the existence of the First Temple from the fourth regnal year of Solomon until its destruction in the eleventh regnal year of Zedekiah, which according to the Deuteronomistic History is exact 430 years. However, in that case it would be not possible to regard 40 years as corresponding to the reign of Solomon.

this case Pekah reigned for only four years – something which can easily be put in harmony with the Assyrian documents. This being the case we have the following synchronisms:

Uzziah 52	= Pekah 1	2 Kgs 15.27
Ahaz 1	= Pekah 2	
Ahaz 3	= Pekah 4	
Ahaz 4	= Hosea 1	

What still remains obscure are the synchronisms Ahaz 12 = Hosea 1 (2 Kgs 17.1), Hezekiah 1 = Hosea 3 (2 Kgs 18.1-2) as well as Hezekiah 4 = Hosea 7 and Hezekiah 6 = Hosea 9 (2 Kgs 18.9-11). If we calculate from Ahaz 12 = Hosea 1 we receive the following list of synchronisms:

Jotham 20 = Ahaz 12	= Hosea 1
Ahaz 16 = Hezekiah 1	= Hosea 5
Hezekiah 4	= Hosea 8
Hezekiah 6	= Hosea 10

It becomes clear that Ahaz 12 = Hosea 1 is not in harmony with other synchronisms in 2 Kgs 15.30; 17.1; 18.1-2, 9-11. These synchronisms are all in conflict with each other. We have already established that the synchronism in 2 Kgs 16.1-2 is a later fabrication and should therefore not be our starting-point when we evaluate the above synchronisms in 2 Kgs 15.30; 17.1; 18.1-2, 9-11. Therefore, the essential question is whether we have any historically reliable tradition among these conflicting synchronisms. It is clear that this question is crucial for understanding the biblical chronology of the Judean kings and it seems to me that we cannot present only one alternative to understand these synchronisms.

We have an option that Hezekiah was king when Samaria was destroyed.[19] Calculating from synchronisms in 2 Kgs 18.9-11 backwards we receive the following synchronisms (we assume that our conclusion that Pekah reigned for only 4 years is right; it receives support from Assyrian documents):

Hezekiah 6	= Hosea 9
Hezekiah 4	= Hosea 7
Hezekiah 1 = Ahaz 16	= Hosea 4
Ahaz 13	= Hosea 1
Ahaz 12	= Pekah 4
Ahaz 9	= Pekah 1 = Pekahiah 2
Ahaz 8	= Pekahiah 1 = Menahem 10
Ahaz 1	= Menahem 3

19. So e.g. Begrich, *Chronologie*; Jepsen, 'Zur Chronologie'; Hayes and Hooker, *New Chronology*, pp. 56-67; Galil, *Chronology of the Kings of Israel and Judah*, pp. 83-97.

3. Reliability of the Synchronic Tradition

The synchronism Ahaz 1 = Menahem 3 would imply that Ahaz became king in Uzziah 41, and that Jotham's 16-year reigning period should be dated to Uzziah 26 – Uzziah 41.

On the other hand, if we assume that there was an older pre-Deuteronomistic tradition according to which Ahaz became king immediately after Uzziah in Pekah's 2nd regnal year and if Pekah reigned for only 4 years – as we have argued above – then we receive the following synchronisms:

> Ahaz 1 = Pekah 2
> Ahaz 3 = Pekah 4
> Ahaz 4 = Hosea 1
> Ahaz 12 = Hosea 9

Ahaz 12 = Hosea 9 would mean that Hosea was dethroned (not ascended to the throne) in Ahaz's 12th regnal year.[20] This information may have been behind the synchronism in 2 Kgs 17.1. This being the case we must consider the possibility that Ahaz was king in Judah when Samaria was destroyed some time during 722–20 BCE according to Assyrian records. This option receives support also from the fact that Sennacherib invaded Judah in Hezekiah's 14th regnal year, which according to Assyrian documents took place in 701 BCE.

In this connection we must deal with Isa. 14.28-32 which has been dated to the year when Ahaz died. In this prophecy the reference is made to the coming destruction of Philistia which will take place when the Assyrian army destroys it:

> Do not rejoice, all you Philistines,
> that the rod that struck you is broken;
> from the root of that snake will spring ($yēṣē'$) up a viper,
> its fruit will be a flying serpent.

This prophecy has been interpreted as supporting the date of 727/26 BCE as the year of enthronement of Hezekiah.[21] The argument is that the rod that struck the Philistines was Tiglath-Pileser III who died in 727 BCE. The prophecy should have warned the Philistines not to rejoice about this event because after Tiglath-Pileser III new tyrants would appear.

---

20. The possibility to explain 2 Kgs 17.1 so that behind the synchronism is Hosea's being dethroned in Ahaz' 12th regnal year has been noted earlier by Na'aman ('Kingdoms of Israel and Judah', p. 83).

21. See especially J. Begrich, 'Jes 14, 28-32: Ein Beitrag zur Chronologie der israelitisch-judäischen Königszeit', in W. Zimmerli (ed.), *Joachim Begrich: Gesammelte Studien zum Alten Testament* (TB, 21; Munich: Kaiser, 1964), pp. 121-31. This option is also taken up by Hughes (*Secrets of the Times*, pp. 213-18).

However, there are clearly other ways of interpreting this prophecy. One may also vocalize the verb *yāṣā'* so that it refers to the past time and points out that the rod is Tiglath-Pileser and the snake Shalmaneser V and its fruit is the flying serpent i.e. Sargon II who would destroy Ashdod (Isaiah 20). If this is so then the prophecy of Isa. 14.28-32 could also have been uttered just before the rebellion of Ashdod in 715/14 BCE.

The synchronism in 2 Kgs 15.30 according to which Jotham would have reigned for at least 20 years can also be used to argue that the king who followed Uzziah reigned for 20 years. That king was Ahaz as we have argued above, but some pre-Deuteronomistic writers understood that the king under question must have been Jotham. Thus, if Jotham reigned for only 16 years then we have two alternative traditions: either Jotham reigned for 16 years and Ahaz for 20 years, or alternatively Jotham reigned for 20 years and Ahaz for 16 years.

We have seen that there is no self-evident explanation for the synchronism Ahaz 12 = Hosea 1 because it is not in harmony with other synchronisms and it confuses the whole chronological system of the Judean kings just before the destruction of Samaria. Nevertheless, we have good possibility to explain theologically why the destruction of Samaria has later been dated to the reign of Hezekiah. The miraculous salvation of Jerusalem during the time of Hezekiah was contrasted to the destruction of Samaria (2 Kgs 18.34-35; Isa. 36.19-20; see also Isa. 10.10-12).[22] By dating the destruction of Samaria to the reign of Hezekiah, the Deuteronomist wanted to emphasize the contrast between the illegitimate northern kings and the legitimate Davidic king who turned to Yahweh and who worshipped him only in Jerusalem (2 Kgs 18.4, 22). One option could be that the synchronism Ahaz 12 = Hosea 1 originally referred to *the dethronement of Hosea in Ahaz's twelfth regnal year*. The Deuteronomist (or someone before him) apparently had problems in understanding the synchronism after the reign of Uzziah. He found it was possible to date the destruction of Samaria to the reign of Hezekiah and fabricated the synchronism Ahaz 12 = Hosea 1.

Summary

It is important to emphasize that so far we have not connected any reign of the Judean or Israelite king to actual chronology. We have demonstrated that it is possible to argue for a relatively coherent system of

---

22. See A. Laato, '*About Zion I will not be silent': The Book of Isaiah as an Ideological Unity* (ConBOT, 44; Stockholm: Almqvist & Wiksell International, 1998), pp. 66-125.

synchronisms by considering only the biblical data. We have explained how the conflicting synchronisms in the Bible have been generated. This means that the Deuteronomist knew different traditions and that he has partly reworked them. We also noted that in the reigns of Hezekiah and Ahaz there are several synchronisms which are difficult to interpret. This situation correlates well with the fact that in Hezekiah's time two historical events, namely the destruction of Samaria and the invasion of Sennacherib, have been dated to his 6th and 14th regnal year respectively, and that these datings form conflicting chronological data with the Assyrian documents which give 20 years between these two events.

In order to connect the reigns of the Israelite and Judean kings to our modern chronological system the best way is to begin with the last kings of Judah. After all, the Deuteronomist collected traditions at the beginning of the exile and there is good reason to believe that he was well aware of the chronology of the last Judean kings. A good starting-point is the Babylonian Chronicle which gives us some important fixed dates. Another important case is the double dating in Ezek. 1.1-3 which enables us to see how an early biblical editor understood the chronological system of the last Judean kings. These two cases are the task of the next Chapter 4.

4

THE CHRONOLOGY OF THE LAST JUDEAN KINGS

In Chapter 3 we dealt with three problematic periods from the time prior to the destruction of Samaria and demonstrated how we can understand the outcome of some conflicting chronological data in the book of Kings. What we did not do in Chapter 3 was to fix the reigns of the Israelite and Judean kings to our Western chronology. This is our task in this chapter and the following chapter.

In the books of Kings the fall of Samaria provides an important turning-point in chronological data. There are no longer any synchronisms but only chronological information concerning the length of the reigns of the Judean kings. Our aim in this Chapter is to fix the history of the last Judean kings to our Western chronology. The best way to do this is to focus on those historical events which took place at the end of the Judean kingdom, and to fix them to our chronological system. This is a methodologically relevant task because the Babylonian Chronicler gives us some accurate dates which can be used to fix the events which, in the books of Kings, are related to the last Judean kings. Another important chronological system which we shall deal with in this chapter is the period of thirty years at the beginning of the book of Ezekiel (Ezek. 1.1-3). We shall argue that this 'thirty years' is calculated from Josiah's reform and it illustrates how an early exilic editor interpreted the chronology of the last Judean kings.

The Evidence of the Babylonian Chronicle

The Babylonian Chronicle gives three important dates for the biblical events which help us to date the reigns of the last Judean kings. The first event took place in Nabopolassar's 17th regnal year (Nisan 609–Nisan 608) when the Assyrian king Ashur-uballit II attempted to take over Harran with the aid of the Egyptian army (from Tammuz to Elul). This

4. *The Chronology of the Last Judean Kings* 51

being the case, the invasion of the Egyptian army must have taken place in the month of Tammuz (the 4th month) or in the previous month Sivan, which means that the death of Josiah accounted for in 2 Kgs 23.29-30 must have taken place at the end of Sivan or in Tammuz in 609 BCE. This question, in turn, implies that the three-month reign of Shallum must be dated in 609 BCE, presumably to the months Ab, Elul and Tishri or alternatively to Tammuz, Ab and Elul.

Another important date is the battle of Carcemish which took place in Nabopolassar's 21st regnal year (Nisan 605–Nisan 604) in the year of Nebuchadnezzar's accession. Because Nabopolassar died on this year on the month Ab (the fifth month), Nebuchadnezzar returned to Babylon and ascended the royal throne on the first day of the month Elul. He then returned to Hattu (Syria) and was victorious until the month of Shebat (the eleventh month). This being the case the battle of Carchemish took place between Nisan 605 and Ab 605.[1]

The third fixed date which is important for the biblical events is the conquest of Jerusalem in Nebuchadnezzar's 7th regnal year, in Adar 2, which corresponds to the date 16 March 597 BCE.

When we attempt to relate these three fixed dates to the biblical chronology we must take stand to some elementary questions. The first important question is the accession-year. Is there any evidence that accession-year system was followed in Judah? I think the answer is 'yes'. Between Tishri 609 BCE and Adar 597 BCE there are more than eleven years, and therefore Jehoiakim's 11-year reign must have been calculated so that Tishri 609–Tishri 608 BCE was his accession year, and so Tishri 598–Tishri 597 BCE began his 11th regnal year, which was followed by the three-month reign of Jeconiah in Kislev 598–Adar 597 BCE. If we follow the accession-year system backwards we can calculate that Josiah was king in 641/40–610/09, Amon in 643/42–641/40 and Manasseh 697/96–643/42 which corroborates well with the end of the reign of Hezekiah as we shall see later in Chapter 5. This being the case we may assume that the accession-year system was followed in Judah during the period when there were no synchronisms to the reigns of the Israelite kings. This being the case, the reign of Zedekiah must be dated so that Tishri 598–Tishri 597 was his accession year and the year Tishri 597–Tishri 596 his first regnal year. In this way his eleventh regnal year was Tishri 587–Tishri 586.

---

1. Wiseman, *Chronicles of Chaldean Kings*, pp. 23-28, 46, 66-69; A.K. Grayson, *Assyrian and Babylonian Chronicles*, pp. 19-20, 99.

The battle of Carchemish has been dated to Jehoiakim's 4th regnal year (Jer. 46.2) which does not fit the system presented above because Tishri 606–Tishri 605 was his 3rd regnal year. On the other hand, we do not know whether the date in Jer. 46.2 is calculated according to the accession-year or non-accession-year system. According to the non-accession-year system, the date fits in well with the chronological construction presented above.[2]

The following table lists the events accounted for in the Babylonian chronicles and presents how the regnal years of the last Judean kings should be dated.[3]

Nabopolassar 17	Nisan 609–Nisan 608	Death of Josiah at latest in Sivan
	Tishri 609–Tishri 608	Shallum, Jehoiakim became king
Nabopolassar 18	Nisan 608–Nisan 607	
	Tishri 608–Tishri 607	Jehoiakim 1
Nabopolassar 19	Nisan 607–Nisan 606	
	Tishri 607–Tishri 606	Jehoiakim 2
Nabopolassar 20	Nisan 606–Nisan 605	
	Tishri 606–Tishri 605	Jehoiakim 3
Nabopolassar 21	Nisan 605–Nisan 604	Carchemish-battle between Nisan and Ab
	Tishri 605–Tishri 604	Jehoiakim 4
Nebuchadnezzar 1	Nisan 604–Nisan 603	Sack of Ashkelon in Kislev
	Tishri 604–Tishri 603	Jehoiakim 5
Nebuchadnezzar 2	Nisan 603–Nisan 602	
	Tishri 603–Tishri 602	
Nebuchadnezzar 3	Nisan 602–Nisan 601	
	Tishri 602–Tishri 601	
Nebuchadnezzar 4	Nisan 601–Nisan 600	Babylonia failed to conquer Egypt in Kislev
	Tishri 601–Tishri 600	
Nebuchadnezzar 5	Nisan 600–Nisan 599	
	Tishri 600–Tishri 599	

---

2. Of course those who regard the regnal year to lap between the months of Nisan have no problem in regarding Nisan 608–Nisan 607 as Jehoiakim's first regnal year and then Nisan 605–Nisan 604 as his fourth regnal year, which is identical with Nabopolassar's 21st regnal year. So e.g. Kutsch, 'Das Jahr der Katastrophe: 587 v. Chr.'

3. Concerning this see especially Malamat's article 'The Twilight of Judah: In the Egyptian-Babylonian Maelstorm', republished in A. Malamat, *The History of Biblical Israel* (Leiden: Brill, 2004), pp. 299-321.

4. *The Chronology of the Last Judean Kings* 53

Nebuchadnezzar 6	Nisan 599–Nisan 598	Babylonia attacked against Arabs in Kislev
	Tishri 599–Tishri 598	Jehoiakim 10
Nebuchadnezzar 7	Nisan 598–Nisan 597	Conquest of Jerusalem Adar 2 (= March 16)
	Tishri 598–Tishri 597	Jehoiakim 11, Jeconiah and Zedekiah 0
Nebuchadnezzar 8	Nisan 597–Nisan 596	
	Tishri 597–Tishri 596	Zedekiah 1
Nebuchadnezzar 9	Nisan 596–Nisan 595	Babylonia against Elam, Kislev-Tebet
	Tishri 596–Tishri 595	
Nebuchadnezzar 10	Nisan 595–Nisan 594	
	Tishri 595–Tishri 594	
Nebuchadnezzar 11	Nisan 594–Nisan 593	
	Tishri 594–Tishri 593	
Nebuchadnezzar 12	Nisan 593–Nisan 592	
	Tishri 593–Tishri 592	
Nebuchadnezzar 13	Nisan 592–Nisan 591	
	Tishri 592–Tishri 591	
Nebuchadnezzar 14	Nisan 591–Nisan 590	
	Tishri 591–Tishri 590	
Nebuchadnezzar 15	Nisan 590–Nisan 589	
	Tishri 590–Tishri 589	
Nebuchadnezzar 16	Nisan 589–Nisan 588	
	Tishri 589–Tishri 588	
Nebuchadnezzar 17	Nisan 588–Nisan 587	
	Tishri 588–Tishri 587	Zedekiah 10
Nebuchadnezzar 18	Nisan 587–Nisan 586	
	Tishri 587–Tishri 586	Zedekiah 11
Nebuchadnezzar 19	Nisan 586–Nisan 585	
	Tishri 586–Tishri 585	

Against the background of the Babylonian Chronicle we can now deal with the double dating in Ezek. 1.1-3 which reveals how an early editor of the book of Ezekiel understood the chronological dates of the last Judean kings.

The Double Dating in Ezekiel 1.1-3 and the Last Kings of Judah

One key to fix the exact regnal years of the last Judean kings is found at the beginning of the book of Ezekiel, which refers to a thirty-year period which is not fixed in any historical event. We shall argue in this section that this mysterious double dating in Ezek. 1.1-3 can be related to the reform of Josiah. This argument, in turn, gives the possibility to explain how the Tishri Calendar was used to calculate the regnal years of Zedekiah, whereas the Nisan calendar was used to calculate the years of the exiled Jeconiah. We shall begin by analysing Ezek. 1.1-3:

> In the thirtieth year, in the fourth month on the fifth day, while I was among the exiles by the Kebar River, the heavens were opened and I saw visions of God. (2) On the fifth of the month—it was the fifth year of the exile of King Jehoiakin—(3) the word of Yahweh came to Ezekiel the priest, the son of Buzi, by the Kebar River in the land of the Chaldeans. There the hand of Yahweh was on him.

This double dating has been explained in many different ways.[4] The principal theories are as follows:

1. The first date is calculated from the beginning of the Samarian exile. This purely hypothetical assumption has inspired scholars to speculate on whether the content of the book of Ezekiel partially reflects the criticism of Manasseh's religious policy.[5]
2. The figure 30 refers to the age at which Ezekiel was called as a prophet.[6] This explanation is also purely hypothetical.
3. The first date refers to Ezekiel's final prophecies, or to their editing and publication.[7] This theory receives no support from the present form of Ezek. 1.1-3, where Jeconiah's[8] fifth year in captivity is identified as this 30th year.[9]

---

4. A detailed survey of these different proposals can be found in B. Lang, *Ezechiel: Der Prophet und das Buch* (EdF, 153; Darmstadt: Wissenschaftliche Buchgesellschaft, 1981); Zimmerli, *Ezekiel 1*, pp. 112-14; E. Kutsch, *Die Chronologischen Daten des Ezechielbuches* (OBO, 62; Freiburg: Universitätsverlag, 1985), pp. 46-49.

5. See, e.g., C.C. Torrey, *Pseudo-Ezekiel and the Original Prophecy* (Yale Oriental Series Researches, 18; New Haven: Yale University Press, 1930; repr. New York, 1970).

6. See, e.g., K. Budde, 'Zum Eingang des Buches Ezechiel', *JBL* 50 (1931), pp. 20-41; S.G. Taylor, 'A Reconsideration of the "Thirtieth Year" in Ezekiel 1:1', *Tyndale Bulletin* 17 (1966), pp. 119-20. Cf. also NIV: 'In my thirtieth year'.

7. See W.F. Albright, 'The Seal of Eliakim and the Latest Preexilic History of Judah with Some Observations on Ezekiel', *JBL* 51 (1932), pp. 77-106, esp. 97; Zimmerli, *Ezekiel 1*, p. 114; Lang, *Ezechiel*, pp. 19-20; Kutsch, *Die Chronologischen Daten des Ezechielbuches*, p. 50.

8. I prefer to write Jeconiah instead of Jehoiakin.

9. Scholars have often noted that Ezek. 1.1-3 has been reworked. This may be true, but in the present form of the text the thirtieth year in verse 1 is clearly identified with the fifth year of Jeconiah's captivity. This is the double dating which we later explain in this chapter.

4. *The Chronology of the Last Judean Kings* 55

4. Several scholars have suggested a possible textual conjecture to this passage.[10] Such a solution is legitimate only when other possible interpretations are excluded.
5. Finally there are scholars who accept the ancient explanation found in the Targum inasmuch as the first date is calculated from the beginning of Josiah's reform.[11] The aim of this article is to show that this explanation can indeed be confirmed by chronological details from the Old Testament, which, if true, has interesting implications for the chronological system of the book of Ezekiel.[12] The Targum translates Ezek. 1.1 as follows:[13]

> It was in the thirtieth year, *from the time that Hilkiah the High Priest found the Book of Torah in the Temple, in the court under the entrance; during the night, after the beginning of moonlight: in the days of Josiah son of Amon king of the tribe of the House of Judah*; on the fifth day of the month *of Tammuz. The prophet said*: I was among the exiles on the river Chebar, the heavens opened and I beheld, *in the prophetic vision that rested upon me*, a vision *of the glory of the Shekinah* of the Lord.

At the end of this Chapter, a chronological table is presented to enable my readers to follow the arguments offered here. The double dating in Ezek. 1.1-3 connects the two different calendar systems: the Judean system which was based on the Tishri calendar and the Babylonian system which was followed by the exilic community of Jeconiah and which was based on the Nisan-calendar. This bi-partite calendar system explains why the destruction of Jerusalem on the one hand was dated to Jeconiah's 12th regnal year (Ezek. 33.21) and on the other hand to Zedekiah's 11th regnal year (2 Kgs 25.8).

---

10. See these proposals within Kutsch, *Die Chronologischen Daten des Ezechielbuches*, pp. 46-47.

11. So, e.g., J. Herrmann, *Ezechiel* (KAT, 11; Leipzig and Erlangen: Deichert, 1924), p. 10.

12. It is worth noting that scholars frequently argue that the reference to Josiah's reform (often dated to 621 BCE) implies that Ezekiel's calling must be dated to 591 BCE. See, e.g., Taylor, 'A Reconsideration', p. 119; C.F. Whitley, 'The "Thirtieth" Year in Ezekiel I 1', *VT* 9 (1959), pp. 326-30. Kutsch (*Die Chronologischen Daten des Ezechielbuches*, p. 47) argues against the interpretation that the 'thirtieth' refers to Josiah's reform, by observing that if so, the calling of the prophet took place in 593/92 and not in 594/93 BCE. These scholars have not taken into consideration that the regnal years are from Tishri to Tishri, and that the year of the reform should be calculated as year 1. In addition we should note that there is no *prima facie* knowledge that the reform should be dated to 621 BCE.

13. See the translation from S.H. Levey, *The Targum of Ezekiel* (The Aramaic Bible, 13; Wilmington: Michael Glazier, 1987), p. 20.

The information in the Babylonian Chronicle indicates that the battle of Megiddo should be dated approximately in Sivan at the beginning of Nabopolassar's 17th year (calculated from Nisan).[14] This information implies that Shallum's three-month reign could – in principle – overlap with the end of Josiah's 31st official regnal year, i.e. during Tammuz-Ab-Elul. The first year of Jehoiakim's reign could therefore be calculated from Tishri in Nabopolassar 17 and not from Tishri in Nabopolassar 18 as suggested by Malamat.[15] Kutsch has emphasized that Malamat's postdating of Jehoiakim 1 to Nabopolassar 18 is impossible, because Joahaz's (or Shallum's) three-month reign must have ended before Tishri, assuming that Josiah died already in Sivan (the third month).[16] However, the Babylonian Chronicle records that Ashur-uballit II attacked Harran in Tammuz and that this battle lasted until the month Elul. What is not stated clearly is the point at which the Egyptian army appeared to assist the Assyrian army. Was it at the end of Tammuz or at the beginning of the month? In any case it seems reasonable to assume that Shallum could not have been dethroned until the Egyptian army returned from Harran. The dethronement must have taken place at the latest in the following month after Elul which is Tishri. This being the case we can conclude that Jehoiakim became king after the new year in Tishri and therefore Tishri 608–Tishri 607 must be his first regnal year and the preceding year his accession year.

14. The Egyptian army was stationed in Harran during Tammuz-Elul, indicating that Necho had marched through Megiddo in the month of Sivan or Tammuz. See Wiseman, *Chronicles of Chaldean Kings*, pp. 19-20, 45, 62-63. According to the Babylonian Chronicle 'in the month of Tammuz Aššur-uballit, king of Assyria, a great Egyptian army...crossed the river and marched against the city of Harran to conquer it' (p. 63). See also Grayson, *Assyrian and Babylonian Chronicles*, pp. 18-19, 96.

15. See Malamat, 'The Last Kings of Judah', pp. 140-41; Malamat, 'The Twilight of Judah in the Egyptian-Babylonian Maelstrom', in J.A. Emerton (ed.), *Congress Volume: Edinburgh 1974* (VTSup, 28; Leiden: Brill, 1975), pp. 123-45 [reproduced in Malamat, *History of Biblical Israel*, pp. 299-321]. Malamat writes (*History of Biblical Israel*, p. 303) that 'Jehoiakim apparently came to the throne only in Tishri 609 B.C.'

16. Kutsch *Die chronologischen Daten des Ezechielbuches*, pp. 15-19. Kutsch writes: 'Ob der Wechsel der Königsjahre im Frühjahr oder im Herbst liegt: Seine Regierungszeit hat das nächste Neujahr nicht erreicht...' It is worth noting that on p. 13 Kutsch writes: 'Wenn Necho im 4. bis 6. Monat in Assyrien war, ist er wohl im 3. Monat an Juda vorbezeigen; in diese Zeit – d.h. etwa Mai/Juni – fällt der Tod Josias. Auf seinem Rückweg nach Egypten im 6. oder 7. Monat hat Necho den Joahas nach Ägypten verschleppt'. In that case Jehoiakim's enthronement could have occurred after Tishri 1.

4. *The Chronology of the Last Judean Kings*   57

Vogt comments that the beginning of Jeconiah's captivity should be dated to Nebuchadnezzar 8 because Jerusalem was captured at the end of Nebuchadnezzar 7 (viz. on 2 Adar) and both 2 Kgs 24.12 and 2 Chron. 36.10 emphasize that Jeconiah was deported only in the following year i.e. in Nebuchadnezzar 8.[17] This view seems to receive support from the fact that according to 2 Kgs 25.9; Jer. 52.12, Jerusalem was destroyed in Nebuchadnezzar 19, corresponding to the date in Ezek. 33.21, which implies that news of this event reached Ezekiel in the 10th month of Jeconiah 12 (= Nebuchadnezzar 19). However, Kutsch has rightly noted that the Babylonian Chronicle connects the deportation of the exiles during the time of Jeconiah to Nebuchadnezzar's 7th regnal year:[18]

> The seventh year: In the month of Kislev the king of Akkad mustered his army and marched Hattu. He encamped against the city of Judah and on the second day of the month Adar he captured the city (and) seized (its) king. A king of his own choice he appointed in the city (and) taking the vast tribute he brought it into Babylon.

Indeed, Jer. 52.28-30 date the first exile to Nebuchadnezzar's 7th and the destruction of Jerusalem to Nebuchadnezzar's 18th regnal year, indicating that in Judah there were two different ways of calculating Nebuchadnezzar's regnal years. This fact can be explained in different ways. One possibility could be that both accession-year and non-accession-year systems were in use. However, this is perhaps not the best way to explain the case, because there is reason to suggest that Jerusalem was destroyed in Nebuchadnezzar's 19th regnal year. The better alternative is that the Judean editor found relating the Babylonian Nisan calendar system to the Judean Tishri calendar system problematic. Zedekiah's 11th regnal year (Tishri 587–Tishri 586) overlaps both Nebuchadnezzar's 18th and 19th regnal years. The dating of the first conquest of Jerusalem and the exile of Jeconiah to the 7th and 8th regnal years can easily be explained as the exile having taken place at the very end of the 7th regnal year. This reasoning, in turn, implies that Jeconiah's first year of captivity was calculated from Nebuchadnezzar's 7th regnal year, i.e. from Nisan 597 to Nisan 596 when Jeconiah surrendered to the Babylonians.

17. E. Vogt, 'Die Neubabylonische Chronik über die Schlacht bei Karkemisch und die Einnahme von Jerusalem', in *Volume du Congrès Strassbourg 1956* (VTSup, 4; Leiden: Brill, 1956), pp. 67-96 (92-94). So also Malamat, 'Last Kings', pp. 144-45.
18. Kutsch, 'Das Jahr der katastrophe: 587 v. Chr.', pp. 520-43 [reprinted in E. Kutsch, *Kleine Schriften zum Alten Testament zum 65. Geburtstag* (ed. L. Schmidt and K. Eberlein; BZAW, 168; Berlin: W. de Gruyter, 1986), pp. 3-28, esp. 8-9]. The quotation of the Babylonian Chronicle is from Grayson, *Assyrian and Babylonian Chronicles*, p. 103.

Kutsch regards 2 Kgs 24.12 and 2 Chron. 36.10 (which refers to the turn of the year, *tešūbat haššānâ*) as proof that the regnal years in Judah were changed during Nisan and not in Tishri.[19] However, these details together with the Babylonian Chronicle merely indicate that the regnal year of the Babylonian king changed in Nisan. 2 Chron. 36.10 is from the later Persian period and only shows that the Babylonian calendar – according to which the turn of the religious year occurred in Nisan – was adopted in Judah, and that it was thus possible to speak of *tešūbat haššānâ* in Nisan. In the rabbinic literature it is customary to record the turn of the official year in Tishri and the turn of the religious year in Nisan (*m. Rosh Hashanah* 1.1).

The first dating in Ezek. 1.1-3 follows the Tishri calendar (because it refers back to Judean regnal years) while Jeconiah's exile was calculated according to the Nisan-calendar – a solution which plausibly was relevant in the Babylonian exile. Thus the 30th year in Ezek. 1.1 corresponds to the year from Tishri in Zedekiah 5 to Tishri in Zedekiah 6. Thus we deduce that, according to the calendar system in Ezek. 1.1, the first year corresponds to the year from Tishri in Josiah 18 to Tishri in Josiah 19. Josiah's reformation is dated to this period, and according to 2 Kgs 23.21-23, the Passover festival took place in the middle of Josiah's 18th regnal year (calculated from Tishri to Tishri). This being the case we have good reason to regard the date in Ezek. 1.1 as corresponding to the religious calendar year calculated from Tishri in Josiah 18 to Tishri in Josiah 19, when the Deuteronomic reformation was implemented in Jerusalem.

If we assume that the sabbatical years came to be calculated from the beginning of Josiah's reform (cf. Deut. 15) then we find that the utopian vision in Ezekiel 40–48 is dated to the 25th year of Jeconiah's exile which corresponds to the 50th year after Josiah's reform (Ezek. 40.1):

> In the twenty-fifth year of our exile, at the beginning of the year, on the tenth of the month, in the fourteenth year after the fall of the city — on that very day the hand of the LORD was on me and he took me there.

According to the dating of Ezek. 40.1 the prophet had his great vision concerning the Temple of Jerusalem at the beginning of the year, on the tenth day. Kutsch interprets this dating as Nisan 10th.[20] However, the Hebrew expression *berō'š haššānâ be'āśôr* can easily be interpreted as describing Tishri 10. This is a particularly relevant option when the dating in Ezek. 40.1 refers to the 50th year from Josiah's reform. According

---

19. Kutsch, *Die chronologischen Daten*, p. 19.
20. Kutsch, *Die chronologischen Daten*, pp. 33-36.

to Lev. 25.8-10 it was exactly on Tishri 10th that the Jubilee, i.e. the 50th year, would be announced:

> 8 Count off seven Sabbath years – seven times seven years – so that the seven sabbath years amount to a period of forty-nine years. 9 Then have the trumpet sounded everywhere on the tenth day of the seventh month; on the Day of Atonement sound the trumpet throughout your land. 10 Consecrate the fiftieth year and proclaim liberty throughout the land to all its inhabitants. It shall be a jubilee for you; each of you is to return to your family property and to your own clan.

Furthermore, the dating in Ezek. 40.1 states that the vision was received in the fourteenth year after the fall of the city. This statement corresponds well to the schedule presented in the Table (see below). In this case Jeconiah's 25th year was Nisan 574–Nisan 573 and in that year on Tishri 10, Ezekiel received his vision concerning the future of Jerusalem and its Temple. In the same year, on Tishri 1, the fiftieth year calculated from Josiah 18 began, and it was also the fourteenth year after the destruction of the Temple.

We may assume that Ezekiel, who was a priest (or the editors of his book who were certainly interested in the priestly traditions later published in the Torah) regarded the tradition of Josiah's reform as important. Therefore, they also included the dating system which was fixed to the 18th regnal year of Josiah in the book of Ezekiel. The fact that the great vision of Ezekiel 40–48 was dated to the Jubilee calculated from the reform of Josiah indicates that Josiah's measures to concentrate all cultic activity to Jerusalem prepared the way for the coming restoration of the Judean society.[21] Indeed, Ezekiel 40–48 deals not only with the restoration of Jerusalem and its Temple but also the restoration of the whole land (Ezek. 47) – as envisaged in the law of Jubilee according to Leviticus 25. It is also worth noting that the argument in Ezek. 46.17 is based on Jubilee (see Lev. 25.10).

One may wonder why Josiah is not mentioned in the book of Ezekiel if his reform was so crucial for the dating of Ezek. 1.1-3. I have argued elsewhere that Josiah plays a significant role in the redactional unity of Ezekiel 17–19.[22] The book of Ezekiel contains severe criticism of both Zedekiah and his full brother Shallum. This stance differs markedly from

---

21. Cf. also J.S. Bergsma, 'The Restored Temple as "Built Jubilee" in Ezekiel 40–48', *Proceedings of the Eastern Great Lakes and Midwest Biblical Society* 24 (2004), pp. 75-85.

22. See A. Laato, *Josiah and David Redivivus: The Historical Josiah and the Messianic Expectations of Exilic and Postexilic Times* (ConBOT, 33; Stockholm: Almqvist & Wiksell International, 1992), pp. 144-204, esp. 171-74.

that reflected in the book of Jeremiah where both sons of Hamutal are portrayed more favorably. Another strong contrast between Ezekiel's and Jeremiah's attitudes to the Davidic kingship is that in Ezekiel the messianic expectations are closely connected with the family of Jeconiah (the best evidence is Ezek. 17.22-24 and its relationship to 17.3-4; cf. also 21.30-32). Jeconiah and his father Jehoiakim, in turn, are severely criticized in the book of Jeremiah (Jer. 22.24-30; 36.30-31). Moreover, an apologetic tendency may be discerned in Ezekiel 17–19 which seek to modify the critical attitude towards Jeconiah and his family that is preserved in the book of Jeremiah. Ezekiel 18 was deliberately inserted between Ezekiel 17 and 19 in order to show that Jeconiah and his family were not excluded from the succession to the throne in Jerusalem, provided that they obeyed Yahweh's commandments. The father–son–grandson trial in Ezekiel 18 in its redactional context depicts the Judean kings, Josiah, Jehoiakim and Jeconiah. This procedure shows that Josiah was regarded as a righteous king by the redactor of Ezekiel 17–19, and that he serves as a typos for the coming Messiah predicted in Ezek. 17.22-24. If this analysis is correct, then the double dating in Ezek. 1.1-3 emphasizes that the family of Jeconiah has a future if it follows the reformatory tendencies of Jeconiah's grandfather, Josiah.

This analysis has given us a firm basis to argue how an early Jerusalemite scribe understood the chronology of the last Judean kings from the reform of Josiah to the exile (see the table on the next page). This analysis enables us to calculate regnal years backward to the problematic 8th century. As we saw in Chapter 3 the crucial question for the Judean kings is the way in which the synchronisms related to the reigns of Ahaz and Hezekiah should be understood.

Cultic Years	Judean regnal years	Capture of Jeconiah	Sabbatical cycles
1	Josiah 18 (Tishri 623–Tishri 622)		I
2	Josiah 19		II
7	Josiah 24		VII/1
8	Josiah 25		I
14	Josiah 31 (Tishri 610–Tishri 609)		VII/2
15	Jehoiakim 0 (Tishri 609–Tishri 608)		I
16	Jehoiakim 1		II
21	Jehoiakim 6		VII/3
22	Jehoiakim 7		I
25	Jehoiakim 10 (Tishri 599–Tishri 598)		IV
26	Jehoiakim 11 = Zedekiah 0 (Tishri 598–Tishri 597)	Jeconiah 1 (Nisan 597–Nisan 596)	V

4. The Chronology of the Last Judean Kings

27	Zedekiah 1		VI
		Jeconiah 2	
28	Zedekiah 2		VII/4
		Jeconiah 3	
29	Zedekiah 3		I
		Jeconiah 4	
30	Zedekiah 4		II
		Jeconiah 5 (Nisan 593–Nisan 592)	
31	Zedekiah 5		III
		Jeconiah 6	
32	Zedekiah 6		IV
		Jeconiah 7	
33	Zedekiah 7		V
		Jeconiah 8	
34	Zedekiah 8		VI
		Jeconiah 9	
35	Zedekiah 9		VII/5
		Jeconiah 10	
36	Zedekiah 10 (Tishri 588–Tishri 587)		I
		Jeconiah 11	
37	Zedekiah 11 (Tishri 587–Tishri 586) = Year 1 after destruction		II
		Jeconiah 12 (Nisan 586–Nisan 585)	
38	Year 2 after destruction		
42	Year 6 after destruction		VII/6
		Jeconiah 17	
43	Year 7 after destruction		I
48	Year 12 after destruction		VI
		Jeconiah 24	
49	Year 13 after destruction		VII/7
		Jeconiah 25 (Nisan 573–Nisan 572)	
50	Year 14 after destruction		**Jubilee**

5

THE ABSOLUTE BIBLICAL CHRONOLOGY OF THE BOOKS OF KINGS

In Chapter 4 we demonstrated how the biblical writers, who must have known the events of the last Judean kings well, related their reigns to the 50 years cycle between 623–573 BCE. In this chapter we shall now relate the biblical synchronisms of the pre-exilic kings and the lengths of the reigns to our modern chronology. It is worth noting that this connection will be made only after we have first tried to argue how certain conflicting synchronisms have been generated.

When Josiah's 18th regnal year is taken as Tishri 623–Tishri 622 (= 623/622) then his first regnal year is 640/39 and accession year 641/40. Amon's two-year reign can be placed to 643/42–641/40 and Manasseh's 55-year reign to 697/96–643/42. If we assume that Hezekiah became king in 715/714 so that his 14th regnal year would correspond to the invasion of Sennacherib in 702/701 then he would have reigned for only 19 years and not 29 years as stated in 2 Kgs 18.1-2. However, there is a plausible explanation as to how the reign of Hezekiah was lengthened from 19 years to 29 years. One explanation is that the number 19 has been read as 29. Another possibility is found in the story in 2 Kings 20 (par Isa. 38) according to which Hezekiah recovered from his illness and thus received an extra 15 years. The story (which was originally not dated) was edited after the destruction of the Assyrian army which took place in Hezekiah's 14th year. The simple calculation 14 + 15 results in 29 years in total. Thus we receive 715/714–697/696 for the reign of Hezekiah.

We argued in Chapter 3 that Ahaz could have reigned for 20 years. In this case his reign should be dated to 735/34–715/14 which correlates nicely to just before the time of the Syro-Ephraimite war.

5. *The Absolute Biblical Chronology*

An important chronological date was established by Na'aman when he argued that Hosea established his kingship only after the Syro-Ephraimite war. Na'aman's plausible proposal thus indicates that the beginning of the reign of Hosea must be dated to 731/30 BCE.[1]

By using the synchronisms which we argued for in Chapter 3 we can now connect the reigns of the Israelite and Judean kings to our Western chronology.

Israel		Judah	
Jeroboam I	930/29–909/08	Rehoboam	930/29–914/13
Nadab	909/08–908/07	Abiam	913/12–910/09
Baasha	908/07–885/84	Asa	910/09–870/69
Elah	885/84–884/83	Jehoshaphat	870/69–847/46
Zimri	884/83	Jehoram	847/46–846/45
Omri	884/83–873/72	Ahaziah	846/45
Ahab	873/72–852/51	Athaliah	845/44–840/39
Ahaziah	852/51–851/50	Joash	840/39–801/00
Jehoram	851/50–845/44	Amaziah	801/00–787/86
Jehu	845/44–818/17	Uzziah	786/85–735/34
Jehoahaz	818/17–802/01	Jotham	750/49–735/34 (2 Kgs 15.5)[2]
Jehoash	802/01–787/86	Ahaz	735/34–716/15[3]
Jeroboam II	787/86–747/46	Hezekiah	715/14–697/96[4]
Zechariah	747/46	Manasseh	697/96–643/42
Shallum	746/45	Amon	643/42–641/40
Menahem	746/45–737/36	Josiah	641/40–610/09
Pekahiah	737/36–735/34	Jehoahaz	609
Pekah	735/34–732/31	Jehoiakim	609/08–598/97
Hosea	731/30–723/22	Jeconiah	598 (Dec)–597 (March)
		Zedekiah	597–587

Constructed Chronology and its Historical Relevance

There are several references in the biblical texts to historical events which can be dated and which are also related to a certain reign of Israelite or Judean kings or to their particular regnal years. We have already referred

---

1. Na'aman, 'Kingdoms of Israel and Judah', pp. 71-92.
2. Another possibility is that Samaria was destroyed in Hezekiah's reigning period, which implies that the whole reigning period of Jotham and a part of the reigning period of Ahaz would be co-regencies in the time of Uzziah. As we noted in Chapter 2 the reigning period of Jotham would in that case be Uzziah 26–Uzziah 41 which correspond to years 760/59–745/44 in our chronology.
3. Alternatively 745/44–725/24.
4. Alternatively 725/24–697/96.

to some of these correspondences but we shall now deal with all parallel dates to extra-biblical texts more systematically.[5]

The Invasion of Shishak

The reign of Shishak can be dated almost accurately and scholars agree that his reign began about 946–944 BCE.[6] Shishak ruled for 21 years and the Palestinian expedition took place at the end of his reign. The option that Shishak ruled from 945–924 BCE or perhaps even 944–923 BCE is therefore plausible. Our chronology gives Rehoboam the years 930/29–914/13 and his fifth regnal year (1 Kgs 14.25) would thus be Tishri 926–Tishri 925. This date would fit in well with the details we know from Egyptian documents, and this fact, in turn, indicates that the historical and chronological data in 1 Kgs 14.25 originates from Jerusalemite royal archives.[7]

The Battle of Qarqar

Shalmaneser III battled at Qarqar against the Palestinian coalition which was under the leadership of Hadad-ezer, the king of Aram. The Assyrian king mentioned that Ahab the king of Israel was among the troops of the coalition: '2,000 chariots and 10,000 troops of Ahab'.[8] The battle took place in spring 853 BCE when, according to our chronology, Ahab was still on throne. The biblical traditions do not mention this battle of Qarqar. Instead they indicate that Ahab died in his battle against Aram (1 Kings 22). There is some doubt among scholars as to whether the events accounted in 1 Kings 20 and 22 can be related to the reign of Ahab because Israel and Aram were apparently in coalition against

---

5. Concerning these parallels between biblical and extra-biblical evidence see especially Tadmor, 'Chronology of the First Temple Period'.

6. For the nature of Egyptian chronology and the reign of Shishak in particularly see R.A. Parker, *The Calendars of Ancient Egypt* (Studies in Ancient Oriental Civilization, 26; Chicago: University of Chicago Press, 1950); K.A. Kitchen, *The Third Intermediate Period in Egypt (1100–650 B.C.)* (Warminster: Aris & Phillips, 1973), pp. 287-302; Kitchen, 'Egypt, History of (Chronology)', *ABD*, II, pp. 322-31. This is contra Albright's view. See Albright, 'Further Light'.

7. See N. Na'aman, 'Israel, Edom and Egypt in the 10th Century B.C.E.', *TA* 19 (1992), pp. 71-93, esp. 83-86; Na'aman, 'Shishak's Campaign to Palestine as Reflected by the Epigraphic, Biblical and Archaeological Evidence', *Zion* 63 (1998), pp. 247-76 (Hebrew). Na'aman concludes that the Deuteronomist had a source while the Chronicler knew only the Deuteronomistic account in 1 Kgs 14.25-28, nothing more.

8. Grayson, *Assyrian Rulers*, p. 23

Assyria at Qarqar in 853 BCE.⁹ According to our chronology, this new battle against Aram would have taken place only one year after the battle of Qarqar. The traditions in 1 Kings 20 and 22 are not annalistic reports but rather prophetic stories (cf. the climax of 1 Kgs 20 in vv. 35-43) transmitted orally for a longer period. One detail in the story, namely 1 Kgs 22.26 where reference is made to Joash (יוֹאָשׁ) the son of the king, has given rise to the speculation that the story originally related to Jehoahaz, whose son was Joash.¹⁰ However, there are problems in this proposal. The son of Jehoahaz has been written יְהוֹאָשׁ. In addition, there is an apparent chronological conflict because the reign of Jehoash is not related to that of Jehoshaphat. We may well assume that Ahab had several sons, not only Ahaziah and Jehoram. Finally, the biblical stories in 1 Kings 20 and 22 are more complex and they do not refer only to the hostile relationship between Aram and Israel. After all 1 Kgs 20.34 *expressis verbis* refers to the agreement of peace between Aram and Israel. I cannot see any problem in the explanation that after the battle of Qarqar, Aram evaluated the situation in such a way that the Assyrian threat was seen to be finally over. Aram's claim to political hegemony in Syro-Palestine renewed hostilities between Aram and Israel, resulting in the battle referred to in 1 Kings 22. Our chronology would allow this historical scenario.

The Tribute of Jehu
In 845 BCE Shalmaneser III made his fourth western campaign against Aram. At this time Hadadezer was still the king of Aram. The situation was different some years later in 841 BCE when the Assyrian king reported on the intern-political strife in Aram in this way:¹¹ 'Hadad-ezer (Adad-idri) passed away (and) Haza'el, son of a nobody, took the throne. He mustered his numerous troops (and) moved against me to wage war and battle. I fought with him (and) defeated him. I took away from him his walled camp. He fled to save his life (and) I pursued (him) as far as Damascus, his royal city'. The historical events parallel the revolt of Jehu in Israel (see 2 Kgs 8.7-15; 9.1-37). In 841 BCE Jehu paid tribute to Shalmaneser III as the famous Black Obelisk accounts for, including a

---

9. The well-written sourcebook for the history of Israel is illustrative in this regard: Miller and Hayes, *History of Ancient Israel and Judah*, p. 262: '...we discount the narratives in question as valid sources of information for the Omride era but will draw upon them as sources for the Jehu period'. See also Hughes, *Secrets of the Times*, pp. 187-89.
10. So, e.g., Hughes, *Secrets of the Times*, pp. 187-89.
11. The translation is from Grayson, *Assyrian Rulers*, p. 118.

scene where Jehu is seen as subjugating to the Assyrian king. Our chronology indicates that the Assyrian attack in 845 BCE (probably in spring-time as usual) was not successful, and gave Aram the opportunity to direct a military attack against the dynasty of Omri in Israel as indicated by the Tel Dan Inscription and 2 Kings 9. These events led to the politically unstable situation in Israel which gave Jehu the possibility to rise to power in the subsequent year 845 (Tishri)–844 (Tishri).[12]

The Tribute of Jehoash
The Rimah Stela of Adad-nirari III was found in 1967 and it contains the name of Jehoash (Iu'asu). The text states that in his campaign against the land of Hatti and Amurru and Damascus, the Assyrian king received tribute from them but also from 'Joash (Iu'asu), the Samaritan, (and) of the people of Tyre (and) Sidon'. The text itself cannot be 'earlier than 797 BC',[13] but more problematic is the date of the tribute of Jehoash. There are chronological frameworks for the paying of the tribute. At the earliest, it can have taken place in 802 BCE,[14] when according to the Assyrian Eponym list Adad-nirari made a campaign 'to the Sea'. The latest it can have taken place is in 796 BCE[15] when Adad-nirari campaigned against Mansuate in Syria.[16] Our chronology allows both dates.[17]

The Possible Tribute of Azariah/Uzziah
An old *crux interpretum* has been the Calah annals of Tiglath-Pileser III and the fragmentary inscription nr. 19 that mentions Azriyau, however, without any reference to his land (the text is broken just after the name).[18] Scholars have discussed whether the reference is to the king of Judah, Azariah/Uzziah but no consensus has been reached and there is even a proposal that the annals should be dated to the time of Sennacherib.[19] In any case our chronology allows this possible reference to Uzziah because we have argued that Uzziah died only in 735/34 BCE.

12. Both Begrich (*Chronologie*) and Jepsen ('Zur Chronologie') also date the beginning of the reign of Jehu to 845 BCE.
13. Grayson, *Assyrian Rulers*, p. 210.
14. See Jepsen, 'Ein Neuer Fixpunkt, pp. 359-61.
15. Miller and Hayes, *History of Ancient Israel and Judah*, pp. 298-99.
16. Concerning these dates and events see Millard, *The Eponyms of the Assyrian Empires*, pp. 34-35, 57.
17. Concerning the year 802 BCE see, in particular, Jepsen's article 'Ein Neuer Fixpunkt'.
18. See the text in Tadmor, *The Inscriptions of Tiglath-Pileser III*, pp. 58-65, 273-74.
19. See N. Na'aman, 'Sennacherib's "Letter to God" on his Campaign to Judah', *BASOR* 214 (1974), pp. 25-39.

5. *The Absolute Biblical Chronology*

The Tribute of Menahem

According to the Assyrian Eponym list Tiglath-Pileser III conquered Kullani (Calno) in 738 BCE. In this connection he mentions that he received tribute from Rezin (Rahianu) of Damascus and Menahem of Samaria.[20] This tribute is apparently the same which is mentioned in 2 Kgs 15.19-20. Our chronology allows this event because Menahem ruled in 746/45–737/36 BCE.

The Contact of Ahaz to Tiglat-Pileser III

In the so-called Summary Inscription (Nr. 7) of Tiglath-Pileser III it is reported that Jehoahaz (*Ia-u-ha-zi*) of Judah paid tribute to the Assyrian king. The tribute paid is apparently related to the Assyrian invasion against Philistia in 734 BCE or (less probably) against Damascus and Israel in 733–732 BCE. It is not sure – even though I regard it as probable – that the tribute is the same as that accounted in 2 Kgs 16.8-9.[21] Our chronology is in harmony with this dating.

The Dethronement of Pekah and the Accession of Hosea

Two inscriptions of Tiglath-Pileser III refer to the dethronement of Pekah and the installation of Hosea instead of him on the throne of Samaria. The Summary Inscriptions 4:17' is fragmentary and it is possible to reconstruct it so that Tiglath-Pileser himself killed Pekah or that the inhabitants of Samaria did so.[22] Summary Inscription 13 is similarly enigmatic on this point. It is possible to construct the text in such a way that the Israelites killed Pekah.[23] The installation of Hosea on the throne is mentioned twice in the Summary Inscriptions 4:17' and 9:10.[24] These events are related to the Assyrian punishing expedition as a consequence of the Syro-Ephraimite war in 733–732 BCE and therefore must be dated to the year 732/31 BCE as we have already noted earlier in this study by referring to Na'aman's article. These events are in harmony with our chronology – indeed, our construction on this point was partly based on the dates in the Assyrian documents.

---

20. Tadmor, *Inscriptions of Tiglath-Pileser III*, pp. 66-69, 106-107. Tadmor (in collaboration with Mordechai Cogan on pp. 274-76) also presents good arguments against E. Thiele's (*Mysterious Numbers*, pp. 75-98) supposition that Menahem would have paid tribute to Tiglath-Pileser III in 743 BCE when the Assyrian king attacked Arpad.
21. Tadmor, *Inscriptions of Tiglath-Pileser III*, pp. 170-71, 277.
22. Tadmor, *Inscriptions of Tiglath-Pileser III*, pp. 140-41 and esp. p. 141 n. 17.
23. Tadmor, *Inscriptions of Tiglath-Pileser III*, pp. 202-203.
24. Tadmor, *Inscriptions of Tiglath-Pileser III*, pp. 140-41, 188-89.

The Destruction of Samaria

As we have already noted, the destruction of Samaria is a real puzzle for the chronology of the Israelite and Judean kings because the biblical synchronisms of this time are in conflict with each other. Our construction is one possibility and it is based on the fact that the Deuteronomist knew the lengths of the reigns from Zedekiah to Manasseh and that the dating of the invasion of Sennacherib in Judah in 701 BCE to the 14th regnal year of Hezekiah is correct. We have argued that the dating of the destruction of Samaria to the time of Hezekiah is a later chronological construction, the aim of which was to compare the two Assyrian invasions against Samaria and Jerusalem during the reign of the righteous king. While Samaria was destroyed because of its sins, Jerusalem was saved because of its righteous king (2 Kgs 17–19). In any case the chronological data of Judean kings and that of Hosea are problematic, and even though the destruction of the fall of Samaria is dated to the reign of Hezekiah, the synchronisms are not accurate, as has been demonstrated. Therefore, our proposal is that the conflicting synchronisms Ahaz 12 = Hosea 1, Hosea 3 = Hezekiah 1 as well as Hezekiah 4 = Hosea 7 and Hezekiah 6 = Hosea 9 are all later fabrications.

The Invasion of Sennacherib

Our chronology of the late Judean kings after the destruction of Samaria is based on the dating in 2 Kgs 18.13, i.e. that the invasion of Sennacherib in 701 BCE took place in Hezekiah's 14th regnal year.

The Force Labor Tribute of Manasseh to Esarhaddon

Manasseh is listed in the inscriptions of Esarhaddon among the 22 'seacoast and sea kings' who had to assist in building the 'port of Esarhaddon' on the ruins of Sidon. This list must be dated to a time after the destruction of Sidon which took place in Esarhaddon's fourth regnal year i.e. 677 BCE. Because Esarhaddon reigned until 669 BCE it is clear that our chronology is suitable for this extrabiblical information. It is possible that the list of kings refer to the years 677–76 BCE, immediately after the destruction of Sidon.[25]

The Death of Josiah

We have already seen in Chapter 3 that our reconstructed chronology is based on the dating of the death of Josiah in 609 BCE.

---

25. For this see Galil, *Chronology of the Kings of Israel and Judah*, p. 157.

The Battle of Carchemish

As we noted already, in the book of Jeremiah (46.2) the dating of the battle of Carchemish is put in the fourth regnal year of Jehoiakim. Our chronological system gives the fourth regnal year of Jehoiakim the period Tishri 605–Tishri 604 according to the accession year system and Tishri 606–Tishri 605 according to the non-accession year system, and we have argued that Jer. 46.2 followed the later alternative which fits nicely in with the chronological information from the Babylonian Chronicle.[26]

The First Conquest of Jerusalem

According to the Babylonian Chronicle Nebuchadnezzar marched his troops against Judah in his 7th regnal year in the month of Kislev corresponding to December 598 BCE.[27] The city was taken on the second day of the month Adar which probably can be dated to 15th/16th March 597 BCE.[28] Our proposal in this study indicates that Jehoiakim's 11th regnal year is Tishri 599–Tishri 598 and Jeconiah reigned for three months before surrendering to the Babylonian king. In that case Jeconiah's three-month reign can be dated to December 598 BCE–March 597 BCE –which harmonizes well with our chronology. The first official regnal year of Zedekiah was therefore Tishri 598–Tishri 597. Although the chronological details in the Babylonian Chronicle indicate that he was appointed as king in Jerusalem only in 597 BCE, there is nonetheless time to date this event before Tishri 597 BCE when the new year began in Judah. Nevertheless, we must consider the dating in 2 Kgs 24.12 which states that Jeconiah surrendered to the Babylonians in Nebuchadnezzar's 8th regnal year. This statement seems to indicate that in Judah, the regnal years of Nebuchadnezzar were calculated in such a way that his accession year was his first regnal year.

The Destruction of Jerusalem

The beginning of the siege and the destruction of Jerusalem is dated precisely in 2 Kgs 25.1-9 and Jer. 52.4-12:

---

26. It is worth noting that Malamat's chronology presupposes that the battle of Karkemish would have taken place in Jehoiakim's 3rd regnal year. See Malamat, *Biblical Israel*, p. 304 n. 11.

27. Nebuchadnezzar became king during Nabopolassar's 21th regnal year which was Nisan 605–Nisan 604. The Babylonian Chronicle indicates that his first official regnal year was Nisan 604–Nisan 603 and therefore his 7th regnal year must be Nisan 598–Nisan 597.

28. Wiseman, *Chronicles of Chaldean Kings*, pp. 32-35.

> The ninth year of Zedekiah's reign, on the tenth day of the tenth month: Nebuchadnezzar king of Babylon marched against Jerusalem with his whole army.
>
> The eleventh year of King Zedekiah the ninth day of the fourth month: the famine in the city had become so severe that there was no food for the people to eat. The city wall was broken through.
>
> The seventh day [or the tenth day] of the fifth month, in the nineteenth year of Nebuchadnezzar king of Babylon: Nebuzaradan commander of the imperial guard, an official of the king of Babylon, came to Jerusalem. He set fire to the temple, the royal palace and all the houses of Jerusalem.

There are three datings, the first two are made according to the reign of Zedekiah and the last one according to the reign of Nebuchadnezzar. If we begin with the last dating then we find that the 19th regnal year of Nebuchadnezzar is Nisan 586–Nisan 585 BCE. The fifth month corresponds to the month Ab and depending on the dating in 2 Kings or Jeremiah the dating of the destruction of Jerusalem is on 7th or 10th Ab 586 BCE. However, as we noted above, 2 Kgs 24.12 indicates that in Judah the regnal years of Nebuchadnezzar were calculated in such a way that his accession year was his first official regnal year. In that case we must conclude that the dating of 'the seventh day [or the tenth day] of the fifth month, in the nineteenth year of Nebuchadnezzar' corresponds to 7th or 10th Ab 586 BCE. It is worth noting that Jer. 52.29 seems to follow the official Babylonian chronological system when it dates the destruction of Jerusalem to the 18th regnal year. Our chronology nicely allows this dating because Zedekiah's 11th regnal year would be Tishri 587–Tishri 586 BCE. In that case, the siege of Jerusalem would have begun in Zedekiah's 9th regnal year corresponding to Tishri 589–Tishri 588 BCE. The tenth month would be Tebet. This being the case, the following dates can be given:

> The beginning of the siege of Jerusalem: 10th Tebet 588 BCE
> The capture of Jerusalem: 9th Tammuz 586 BCE
> The destruction of Jerusalem: 7th or 10th Ab 586 BCE

Conclusions: Literacy in Israel

What kind of conclusions can be made from the biblical chronological system of the kings of Israel and Judah? First of all we may conclude that everything indicates that this system is based on historically reliable sources from the royal archives. Almost in every problematic synchronism we have been able to demonstrate how it has been generated. Our constructed chronological system corroborates well with the Assyrian and Babylonian historical records and enables us to integrate the biblical events into the larger ancient Near Eastern historical framework. Secondly, because of this good correlation, the only plausible assumption is that the chronological system presented in the books of Kings is based on royal Jerusalemite and Israelite archives. This notion, in turn, indicates that we must assume scribal activities in the Judean and Israelite royal houses from the early monarchic periods onwards. Is such a view relevant in the light of the present research of the Hebrew Bible?

During the last twenty years scholars have increasingly emphasized that in ancient Israel literacy was a relative late phenomenon. They refer to Hebrew epigraphic evidence and conclude that it is only during the 8th century BCE and later that we can speak about literary activity in both administrative and annalistic scribal circles. As far as our topic is concerned, Na'aman's important article from 1992 is quite illustrative. He deals with 'the development of historical writing in Israel'.[29] He wrote that 'no pre-eight century BCE alphabetic inscription has been discovered in the territories of Israel and Judah'.[30] He continues and writes that the Samaria Ostraca as well as Kuntillet 'Ajrud and Balaam plaster inscriptions are the oldest Hebrew inscriptions, dating to from the first half of the eight century BCE, and that they correspond to the earliest recordings of prophecies in the Hebrew Bible. Na'aman concludes that before that time, writing was practiced only in the courts of Jerusalem and Samaria, but there was no audience for whom literacy such as the History of David's Rise to power could have been written.[31] Similar opinions have been presented by other scholars. Israel and Judah did not achieve any considerable degree of literacy before the 8th century BCE.[32]

---

29. N. Na'aman, 'The 'Conquest of Canaan' in the Book of Joshua and in History', in I. Finkelstein and N. Na'aman (eds.), *From Nomadism to Monarchy: Archaeological and Historical Aspects of Early Israel* (Jerusalem: Yad Izhak Ben-Zvi, 1994), pp. 218-81. So also in N. Na'aman, 'Solomon's District List (1 Kings 4:7-19) and the Assyrian Province System in Palestine', *UF* 33 (2001), pp. 419-36.

30. Na'aman, 'Conquest of Canaan', pp. 219-20.

31. Na'aman, 'Conquest of Canaan', pp. 220-21.

32. See, e.g. D.W. Jamieson-Drake, *Scribes and Schools in Monarchic Judah: A Socio-Archaeological Approach* (The Social World of Biblical Antiquity, 9; JSOTSup, 109; Sheffield: Sheffield Academic Press, 1991); H.M. Niemann, *Herrschaft, Königtum und Staat: Skizzen zur soziokulturellen Entwicklung im monarchischen Israel* (FAT, 6; Tübingen: Mohr Siebeck, 1993); W. Dietrich, *Die frühe Königszeit in Israel: 10. Jahrhundert v.Chr* (Biblische Enzyklopädie, 3; Stuttgart: Kohlhammer, 1997); I. Finkelstein and N.A. Silberman, *David and Solomon: In Search of the Bible's Sacred Kings and the Roots of the Western Tradition* (New York: Free Press, 2006), p. 64 and *passim*.

The question of literacy in ancient Israel is essential when we ask whether there were literary presentations of political events with chronological details in the royal archives of early Israelite kingdoms. Recently the question of literacy in early Israel has been dealt with in several studies.[33] All these studies seem to agree that Hebrew became important in the Israelite and Judean societies from about 800 BCE onwards because we have epigraphic evidence for that. The main question is whether we can argue that literacy was important already in the 9th or 10th century or even in pre-monarchic Israel.[34] It seems to me that the answer must be positive. The key arguments are the following.

Seals in Archaeological Excavations
The main tendency in seals is that Hebrew writing appears in them only in the 8th century BCE, not earlier.[35] However, from this evidence it cannot be concluded that the writing system of Hebrew was in its early beginning, because we know that a similar tendency not to use inscribed seals is visible in all ancient Near East.[36] It was only in the 8th century when inscribed seals became more usual. Some inscribed Hebrew seals have been dated to the 9th century.

33. See e.g. W.M. Schniedewind, *How the Bible Became a Book: The Textualization of Ancient Israel* (Cambridge: Cambridge University Press, 2004); D.M. Carr, *Writings on the Tablet of the Heart: Origins of Scripture and Literature* (New York: Oxford University Press, 2011); K. van der Toorn, *Scribal Culture and the Making of the Hebrew Bible* (Cambridge, MA: Harvard University Press, 2007); R.E. Tappy and P.K. McCarter (eds.), *Literate Culture and Tenth-Century Canaan: The Tel Zayit Abecedary in Context* (Winona Lake: Eisenbrauns, 2008); S.L. Sanders, *The Invention of Hebrew* (Urbana and Chicago: University of Illinois Press, 2009); C.A. Rollston, *Writing and Literacy in the World of Ancient Israel: Epigraphic Evidence from the Iron Age* (Atlanta: Society of Biblical Literature, 2010); A. Demsky, *Literacy in Ancient Israel* (The Biblical Encyclopaedia Library, 28; Jerusalem: Bialik Institute, 2012 [Hebrew]).

34. Especially Demsky has emphasized the importance of the alphabet in the development of literacy in the Syro-Canaanite world. While in Egypt and Mesopotamia literacy was limited to the professional scribes (because of the complicated writing system of hieroglyphs and cuneiforms) and thus also to the royal institution, the situation in Syro-Canaanite was different. See further A. Demsky, 'Writing in Ancient Israel Part One: The Biblical Period', in M.J. Mulder (ed.), *Mikra: Text, Translation, Reading and Interpretation of the Hebrew Bible in Ancient Judaism and early Christianity* (Assen/Maastricht: Van Gorcum, 1988), pp. 2-20; Demsky, 'Literacy', in: E.M. Meyers, *The Oxford Encyclopedia of Archaeology in the Near East*, III (Oxford: Oxford University Press, 1997), pp. 362-69.

35. See N. Avigad and B. Sass, *Corpus of West Semitic Stamp Seals* (Jerusalem: The Israel Academy of Sciences and Humanities, 1997).

36. A. Millard, 'Owners and Users of Hebrew Seals', *EI* 26 (1999), pp. 129-33.

Monumental Inscriptions

The Mesha Stele was an official document produced immediately after Moab was released from the yoke of the Kingdom of Israel by the middle of the 9th century BCE. If it was possible to produce such a document in the vassal state of Israel we have good reason to argue that literary activity must also have been developed in Israel at that time. Our only problem in this reasoning is that great monumental inscriptions have not been found...yet. On the other hand, we have a monumental inscription found in Tel Dan (in Aramaic). Even though it is not written in Hebrew, it is reasonable to assume that the Tel Dan inscription implies at the very least foreign scribal praxis in Israel in the 9th and 8th centuries BCE because otherwise it would have been meaningless to write public documents. This reasoning indicates that from the early monarchic period onwards, scribal activity must have existed in Israel and Judah as well.

Early Literary Texts

In recent excavations at Jerusalem Ophel, a fragmentary text has been found which probably originates from an early period of Israel, corresponding to the time of David and Solomon.[37] Another interesting text which may originate from the time of David or Solomon is the Khirbet Qeiyafa text.[38]

Biblical Sources

Na'aman's position that literacy was the privilege of only a few individuals in Israel and Judah is a conclusion which is valid even to later periods. But this conclusion does not imply that literacy could not have had an important role in royal houses – something which Na'aman also accepts. He writes that the practice of literacy was useful for administrative records as well as annalistic references. He also observes elsewhere that later Deuteronomistic writers could not have managed to write about things concerning Shishak if they had not had annalistic archives which they of course interpreted in their own ways.[39] However, we can hardly assume that literacy was only important for those few who

---

37. For this inscription see E. Mazar, D. Ben-Shlomo and S. Ahituv, 'An *Inscribed* Pithos from the *Ophel*', *IEJ* 63 (2013), pp. 39-49.

38. For the discussion of the inscriptions see É. Puech, 'L'ostracon de Khirbet Qeyafa et les débuts de la royauté en Israël', *Revue Biblique* 117 (2010), pp. 162–84; A. Millard, 'The Ostracon from the Days of David Found at Khirbet Qeiyafa', *Tyndale Bulletin* 62 (2011), pp. 1–14; Chr. Rollston, 'The Khirbet Qeiyafa Ostracon: Methodological Musings and Caveats', *TA* 38 (2011), pp. 67–82.

39. See Na'aman, 'Israel, Edom and Egypt', esp. pp. 83-86; Na'aman, 'Shishak's Campaign to Palestine'.

could read. Literacy was also used to produce texts which were read aloud to audiences who could not read. According to Na'aman, the History of David's Rise to power could not have been written in the 10th century BCE Jerusalem because there were no readers. I would evaluate the situation in another way.[40] The texts could easily have been written in order to be read aloud on different occasions where the dynasty of David and Solomon was presented in a favorable way.[41]

Abecedaries

The abecedary found in Tell Zayit indicates that literacy was practiced in early Israel. It is reasonable to regard the abecedary of Tell Zayit as an Israelite exercise of writing activity in the early Iron Age period, probably from 10th century BCE.[42] Discussion seems to concentrate on the question as to whether the abecedary is of Hebrew or Phoenician script. In the case of early Israelite kingdom this is hardly a big problem, because biblical references indicate a close relationship between Jerusalem and Phoenicia. It would be no wonder if literacy was introduced in Israel through these Phoenician contacts. That Phoenician script was known in Canaan a long time before the kingdom of David and Salomon is well demonstrated by the abecedary of Izbet Sartah.[43]

---

40. See also E. Blum, 'Solomon and the United Monarchy: Some Textual Evidence', in: R. Kratz and H. Spieckermann (eds.), *One God – One Cult – One Nation: Archaeological and Biblical Perspectives* (BZAW, 405, Berlin: W. de Gruyter, 2010), pp. 69-78.

41. Concerning the apologetic nature of the text see P.K. McCarter, 'The Apology of David', *JBL* 99 (1980), pp. 489-504; McCarter, ' "Plots, True of False": The Succession Narrative as Court Apologetic', *Interpretation* 35 (1981), pp. 355-67; A. Laato, *A Star Is Rising: The Historical Development of the Old Testament Royal Ideology and the Rise of the Jewish Messianic Expectations* (International Studies in Formative Christianity and Judaism; Atlanta: Scholars Press, 1997), pp. 68-78; B. Halpern, *David's Secret Demons: Messiah, Murderer, Traitor, King* (The Bible in Its World; Atlanta: Scholars Press, 2001).

42. See R.E. Tappy, P.K. McCarter, M.J. Lundberg and B. Zuckerman, 'An Abecedary of the Mid-Tenth Century B.C.E. from the Judean Shephelah', *BASOR* 344 (2006), pp. 5-46; for another evaluation of this abecedary as a Phoenician inscription see Rollston, *Writing and Literacy*, pp. 30-35. Nevertheless, Rollston writes (p. 134) that 'elites in ancient Israel were writing during Iron IIA (900–800 B.C.E.)'. Sanders (*The Invention of Hebrew*, p. 109) regards the Tell Zayit abecedary (and Gezer calendar) as 'representing a pre-Hebrew language and script' but continues 'with no grammatical features and few paleographic signs to distinguish them from Phoenician, they represent a regional, non-bureaucratic writing style that vanishes from Israel and Judah by the eighth century'.

43. See Sanders, *The Invention of Hebrew*, pp. 76-102, esp. 90-96.

* * *

Our study on the chronology of the Israelite and Judean kings indicates that the biblical synchronisms must be based on early literary sources and that this statement is in harmony with the theory that there was literary activity in Israel and Judah from the early monarchic period in the 10th century BCE onwards. It is clear that this dating can be defended by archaeological evidence and inscriptions. This being the case the chronological system in the books of Kings can be used as an argument that older traditions have been preserved in the Hebrew Bible and that some of these traditions can go back even to the time of David and Solomon.

6

THE POSTBIBLICAL CHRONOLOGY AND THE SEVENTY YEARWEEKS IN THE BOOK OF DANIEL

In this Chapter we shall deal with the postexilic chronology of the Jewish people. We shall discuss the seventy yearweeks in Dan. 9.24-27 and show how this 'apocalyptic chronology' has been interpreted as corresponding to the period between the destruction of the First Temple and the Maccabean time, and integrated in the chronological system of Josephus. Josephus misunderstood Dan. 9.24-27 as having described accurately the chronology between the destruction of the First Temple and the Maccabean period. Josephus's solution caused fatal inaccuracy in his chronology. Every subsequent Jewish and Christian attempt to reconstruct the chronology between the destruction of the First Temple and the Second Temple, which was based on Josephus's chronology, had this same inaccuracy.

The second aim of this Chapter is to show that in addition to Josephus, there was another more accurate Jewish chronological system which has been preserved in the writings of Demetrius. This system differs by 27 or 26 years from the accurate chronology. We shall argue that this same Jewish chronology has been used in the Damascus Document as well as in Second (or Syriac) Baruch.

After having presented these two chronological systems we shall show how Dan. 9.24-27 should be interpreted. We shall argue that the numbers in this apocalyptic chronology were never intended to be taken literally as describing accurately the length of the period between the destruction of the First Temple and the Maccabean period. Rather, the numbers were symbolic and corresponded to the chronological data preserved in the Deuteronomistic History.

Inaccurate Chronology in the Second Temple Period

The collapse of the royal infrastructure has left its traces in biblical traditions and chronology. We have very restricted sources on the history of Israel in the Persian and Hellenistic eras, and lack any detailed chronological system which could give us the possibility of dating the postbiblical events accurately. A representative example of this problem is Ezra's coming to Jerusalem. Scholars cannot agree how to date his arrival.[1] The lack of exact chronological information from the exilic and postexilic period is well illustrated by the datings given in Josephus's works. Josephus gives the following inexact chronological data:

First, in *Bell. Jud.* 6.269-270 Josephus dates the period of the buildings of the Temples and the destruction of the Second Temple in the following way: 'From its first foundation by king Solomon up to its present destruction, which took place in the second year of Vespasian's reign, the total period amounts to one thousand one hundred and thirty years seven months and fifteen days; from its rebuilding by Haggai in the second year of the reign of Cyrus until its fall under Vespasian to six hundred and thirty nine years and forty-five days'. Josephus's statement implies that the first year of Cyrus should be dated to 570 BCE. However, Josephus refers here to Haggai who acted in the second year of Darius (Hag. 1.1) which makes it unclear how he had calculated the period of 639 years. From these two figures we receive the length of the period from the foundation of the First Temple to that of the Second Temple as 491 years.

Second, according to *Ant.* 20.234, Josephus calculated the length of the period of the High Priests which he rendered from Jesus son of Josedek (during the time of Cyrus) to the time of Antiochus V Eupator (164–162): 'He and his descendants, fifteen in all, held the office until the reign of Antiochus Eupator; and for four hundred and fourteen years they lived under a democratic form of government'. This implies that the first regnal year of Cyrus was 578 BCE.

Third, according to *Ant.* 13.301, Josephus reckons the period between the return from the exile and Aristobulus I (105–104): 'After their father's death the eldest son Aristobulus saw fit to transform the government into a kingdom, which he judged the best form, and he was the first to put a diadem on his head, four hundred and eighty-one years and

---

1. Two main options for the date of the coming of Ezra have been presented: 458 BCE and 398 BCE. See the discussion about these dates in D.J.A. Clines, *Ezra, Nehemiah, Esther* (NCB; Grand Rapids: Eerdmans, 1984), pp. 14-24.

three months after the time when the people were released from the Babylonian captivity and returned to their own country'. This implies that the first year of Cyrus would be about 586 BCE.

From these three dates referred above Schürer notes that Josephus lengthened the intertestamental period by about 40–50 years.[2] Josephus is not alone here. Schürer notes that similar inaccuracies in chronology are also found in Demetrius's writings. Demetrius, according to the account given in Clement of Alexandria, *Strom.* I.21.141, writes that there were 573 years between the Exile of the ten tribes of Israel in 722–720 BCE and Ptolemaios IV (222 BCE).

In order to understand these inaccuracies it is important to consider the chronological framework of Dan. 9.24-27. It can be shown that Josephus's chronological system is based on Dan. 9.24-27. Daniel 9.24-27 deals with the history of the people of Yahweh in terms of the three apocalyptic epochs which together form the 70-yearweek period. The first epoch is seven yearweeks long and covers the time from the message (of Jeremiah) concerning the return and the rebuilding of Jerusalem to the appearance of the Anointed One. The second period is 62 yearweeks long; during this time Jerusalem is to be restored and rebuilt. The last epoch lasts for one yearweek during which there will be a hard struggle between the assailants of Jerusalem and the people of Yahweh, and which will finally end in victory for Israel.

Scholars agree that the first epoch corresponds to the period between the destruction of Jerusalem and the return from the Exile i.e. 587/86–538 BCE. This timespan also agrees with the length of that period i.e. 7 yearweeks or 49 years. Further, they regard the last epoch as referring

---

2. 'Dass aber ein solcher Irrtum in der Tat möglich ist, beweist aufs schlagendste der Umstand, dass z.B. auch Josephus sich in einem ähnlichen Irrtum befindet, wie aus folgenden drei Stellen hervorgeht: 1) *Bell.Jud.* VI, 4, 8 rechnet er vom zweiten Jahre des Cyrus bis zur Zersörung Jerusalems urch Titus (70 n. Chr.) 639 Jahre. Darnach fiele also das zweite Jahr des Cyrus 569 v. Chr. 2) *Antt.* XX, 10 rechnet er von der Rückkehr aus dem Exil (im ersten Jahre es Cyrus) bis aud Antiochus V. Eupator (164-162) 414 Jahre. 3) *Antt.* XIII, 11, 1 rechnet er von der Rückkehr aus dem Exil (im ersten Jahre des Cyrus) bis auf Aristobul I. (105-104) 481 Jahre. Das Auftreten es Cyrus fiele also nach 1) in d. J. 570 v. Chr., nach 2) etwa in d.J. 578, nach 3) in d. J. 586, während es in Wahrheit in d. J. 537 fällt. Josephus hat also 40-50 Jahre zu viel gerechnet. Noch genauer stimmt mit Daniel der jüdische Hellenist Demetrius überein, der von der Wegführung der zehn Stämme ins Exil bis auf Ptolemäus IV. (222 vor Chr.) 573 Jahre rechnet, also genau wie Daniel um etwa 70 Jahre zuviel (s. die Stelle bei *Clemens Alex. Strom.* I, 21, 141).' See E. Schürer, *Geschichte des jüdischen Volkes im Zeitalter Jesu Christi* (Dritter Band, Vierte Auflage; Leipzig, 1909), pp. 266-67.

to the Maccabean period from about the time of the murder of Onias III (at the end of 170s BCE) to the time of the purification of the Temple (in 164 BCE). This time period corresponds quite well with the length of the last apocalyptical epoch in Dan. 9.24-27, which is one yearweek or 7 years.[3] By interpreting the first and the third epochs in the above-mentioned way scholars get into difficulties, however, over the interpretation of the second epoch. According to Dan. 9.24-27, the second epoch lasts for 62 yearweeks i.e. 434 years, but these years do not fit in between 538 and 170 BCE. This incongruence between 62 yearweeks and the actual years between the return in 538 BCE and the murder of Onias in 170 BCE accounts for the erroneous chronological data in Josephus's writings. We shall now demonstrate how his chronological data have been fabricated.

The Chronology of Josephus

In *Ant.* 20.231-234 Josephus calculates how long the Aaronite high priests held office in the postexilic period from the time of Jesus son of Josedek: 'He and his descendants, fifteen in all, held the office until the reign of Antiochus Eupator; and for four hundred and fourteen years they lived under a democratic form of government'. However, in the following section, *Ant.* 20.235, Josephus states that Antiochus V Eupator (who ruled 164–162 BCE) would have killed 'Onias, surnamed Menelaus'. This statement contradicts what Josephus states elsewhere, namely that it was Antiochus Epiphanes who deposed of the high priestly office (*Ant.* 12.237-241; 15.41). Therefore, we may ask whether Josephus is here dependent on older chronological tradition where Onias refers to the high priest who was murdered by Antiochus Epiphanes. That Josephus first mentions the name 'Onias' and subsequently adds the clarification that he was also called 'Menelaus' make it possible that the figure 414 in the tradition Josephus received refers to the period between the return and the murder of Onias III. This tradition was calculated from Dan. 9.24-27, which – in its present form – refers to the murder of Onias III. Indeed, the Daniel passage confirms that Onias was regarded as the last

---

3. See e.g. the following commentaries: K. Marti, *Das Buch Daniel* (Kurzer Hand-Commentar zum Alten Testament, 18; Tübingen: Mohr, 1901), pp. 72-73; J.A. Montgomery, *A Critical and Exegetical Commentary on the Book of Daniel* (ICC; Edinburgh: T. & T. Clark, 1927), pp. 390-401; N.W. Porteous, *Das Danielbuch* (ATD, 23; Göttingen: Vandenhoeck & Ruprecht, 1962), pp. 115-20; O. Plöger, *Das Buch Daniel* (KAT, 18; Gütersloh: Mohn, 1962), pp. 140-43. See further Koch's survey of research: *Daniel*, pp. 149-54.

legitimate representative of the Aaronite House.[4] How then has the tradition behind *Ant.* 20.234 arrived at this dating? If we assume that the chronology was based on Dan. 9.24-27 and the prophecy of 70 years exile uttered by Jeremiah,[5] then, according to Dan. 9.24-27, there were 69 yearweeks i.e. 483 years between the Exile and the murder of the Anointed One (= Onias III). When the 70 years of captivity prophesied by Jeremiah are deducted from 483, we get 413 years. Because Dan. 9.26 states that 'after the sixty-two yearweeks the Anointed One will be put to death', it has been argued that the murder of Onias III took place in the year 414 after the return. This is exactly the date given by Josephus.

In *Ant.* 13.301 Josephus notes that between the return and Aristobulus I (105–104 BCE) there were 481 years. In a parallel passage *Bell. Jud.* 1.70 the figure is 471 years. These two conflicting dates can be explained as Josephus having had an accurate chronology from the Maccabean times onwards. In that case he knew how many years elapsed between Antiochus Eupator (164–162 BCE) and Aristobulus (105–104 BCE) as well as between Aristobulus I and the murder of Onias III. In the first case we receive $162 - 105 = 57$ and when this figure is added to 414 years we receive 471 years i.e. the exact date given in *Bell. Jud.* 1.70. On the other hand, it is possible that the figure 481 is calculated from the time of Onias' murder, i.e. at the end of the 170s. In this case there were about 67/68 years between that event and Aristobulus I. When this figure is added to 414, we get 481 years, the exact date given in *Ant.* 13.301. This being the case, even this second date is based on the apocalyptical epochs in Dan. 9.24-27.

Finally, we have the date in *Bell. Jud.* 6.270 according to which Josephus allows for 639 years between the second regnal years of Cyrus and the destruction of the Second Temple. Josephus writes:

> From its first foundation by King Solomon up to its present destruction which took place in the second year of Vespasian's reign, the total period amounts to 1130 years 7 months and 15 days; from its rebuilding by Haggai in the second year of the reign of Cyrus until its fall under Vespasian to 639 years 45 days.

---

4. Cf. R. de Vaux, *Ancient Israel. Its Life and Institutions* (Grand Rapids: Eerdmans, 1997), p. 401.
5. In the context Josephus really refers to the prophecy of Jeremiah: 'But after the term of seventy years' captivity under the Babylonians, Cyrus king of Persia, sent the Jews from Babylon to their own land again and gave them leave to rebuild their temple...'

6. *The Postbiblical Chronology*

The figure 639 years is calculated from the tradition that there were 414 years between the return and Antiochus V Eupator (164–162 BCE). With the aid of the accurate chronology from Antiochus Eupator onwards Josephus was able to calculate that there were 234 years to the destruction of the Temple (70 CE). Thus we receive 414 + 234 = 648 years. However, according to Josephus, the temple was not built immediately after the return. In *Ant.* 11.1-30 he states that the enemies of the Jews managed to stop the building of the temple for nine years. This being the case we receive 648 – 9 = 639 which is the figure given by Josephus in *Bell. Jud.* 6.270.

We have seen that Josephus's dating in the three above-mentioned passages is based on Dan. 9.24-27. Therefore Josephus cannot be used as an argument that the chronology during the intertestamental time was confused during the Maccabean period to such a degree that it can clarify why the author of Dan. 9.24-27 overestimated the period between the return and the murder of Onias III by about 70 years. We shall return to this problem of how Dan. 9.24-27 should be interpreted.

Finally it is reasonable to deal with *Bell. Jud.* 6.435-442 which contains the following synchronisms. From the foundation of Jerusalem during the reign of Melchizedek until the destruction of the Second Temple during Titus: 2177 years; from Melchizedek to the destruction of the First Temple during Nebuchadnezzar: 1468 years; from David to the destruction of the First Temple: 477 years and from David to destruction of the Second Temple: 1179 years. From these figures it follows that the period from the destruction of the First Temple to that of the Second Temple lasted for 702 years. This number can be compared with the account in *Bell. Jud.* 6.269-270, according to which there were 639 years between the second building of the Temple and its destruction. Assuming that Josephus calculated the 70 years of captivity between the destruction of the First Temple and the rebuilding of the Second Temple (according to *Bell. Jud.* 6.269-270), 709 years would have elapsed between the destruction of the First Temple and that of the Second Temple. How can this difference of seven years be explained? It is possible to calculate the length of the period between the destruction of the First Temple and that of the Second Temple in *Bell. Jud.* 6.435-442 in another way. There were 2177 years from Melchizedek to Titus and 1468 years from Melchizedek to Nebuchadrezzar which gives us 709 years between the destruction of the two temples. These numbers allow us to argue that Josephus (or his source) in *Bell. Jud.* 6.435-442 miscalculates by seven years. One possibility explanation for this error is that the figure 1179 years was calculated without including David's seven-year reign in Hebron (2 Sam 5.5) while the figure 477 includes that seven-year period.

The Chronology of Demetrius

So far we have dealt with the chronological traditions of Josephus regarding the postexilic period and emphasized that Dan. 9.24-27 plays a central role in them. But how should Demetrius's date of 573 years between the Exile of the northern tribes and Ptolemy IV (who ruled 221–204 BCE) be understood? In *Strom.* I.21.141 Clement of Alexandria writes: '…and from the time that the ten tribes were carried captive from Samaria till Ptolemy the Fourth, were five hundred and seventy-three years, nine months; and from the time that the captivity from Jerusalem took place, three hundred and thirty-eight years and three months'. These two datings imply that there were 235 years between the exiles of the Northern and Southern tribes, which disagrees with the biblical chronological data, according to which there were 135 years between these two events. Samaria was destroyed in Hezekiah's 6th day and we receive the following epochs: Hezekiah 23, Manasseh 55, Amon 2, Josiah 31, Shallum 1 (in fact only three months), Jehoiakim 11, Jeconiah 1 (in fact only three months), Zedekiah 11 = 135. This means that the biblical chronological data give exactly 100 years less than the figure mentioned by Clemens. There is good reason to assume that Demetrius's chronology was based on the biblical sources and that he therefore knew how many years had elapsed between these two exiles. Therefore we must either correct the number 573 to 473 or 338 to 438; in this way we find that the difference between these two numbers is the above-mentioned 135 received from the biblical sources. In the first case the exiles would have occurred in 695 BCE and in 560 BCE respectively, and in the later case 795 BCE and 660 BCE. It is clear that the first alternative is closer to the real dating of these events than the later alternative. Therefore the first alternative is to be preferred, which means that Demetrius's chronology of the intertestamental period is 26/27 years shorter than the real figure and that it differs about 90 years from the chronological system in Dan. 9.24-27.[6]

---

6. Hughes (*Secrets of the Times*, pp. 235-37) has argued that Demetrius after all could have had a reliable chronological tradition. He refers to Demetrius's calculation that between the invasion of Sennacherib and the destruction of Jerusalem there were 128 years and six months and make following assumptions: The figure 128 should be changed to 125 and the figure 573 mentioned above to 473 which means that 338 must be changed to 348 years. This means that the actual error which Demetrius made (for the length of the period 587–222 BCE) was only 17 years. This period of 17 years is the length of the period from the edict of Cyrus (537 BCE) to the refoundation of the temple in the second year of Darius. Then Hughes assumes that Demetrius confused these two events and concludes (p. 237) that 'Demetrius's sources for postexilic chronology must have been completely accurate'.

Because Demetrius lived before the Maccabean era he could not have known Dan. 9.24-27. Therefore his chronological system can help us to clarify other attempts to date events in the postexilic period. It seems to me that the chronological system in the Damascus Document can be explained with the aid of Demetrius's chronology.

The Chronology in the Damascus Document

The Damascus Document divides the history of Israel until the appearance of the Messianic era into four different epochs:
1. The time of wrath after which God established the promised remnant for Israel: 390[7] years (CD I, 5-6).[8]
2. The time of aporia when this remnant lived without a leader: 20 years (CD I, 9-10).
3. The time of the Teacher of Righteousness (CD I, 10ff). In the CD or in the other Qumran scrolls (known today) there is no mention of how long the Teacher of Righteousness served as leader of the community.
4. The time between the death of the Teacher of Righteousness and the Messianic era: about 40 years (*kĕšānîm 'arbā'îm*; CD XX, 13-15).

---

7. The number of the years, 390, originates from Ezek. 4.5. This figure was adopted by the community when it tried to explain its own existence. In addition, the number 390 was thought to contain a mystery concerning the future of Israel. The interpretation arrived at by the community (or probably the Teacher of Righteousness) was that God's wrath lay upon Israel until the holy remnant of the community was established.

8. There is no consensus among scholars on how this first epoch should be interpreted. Some scholars stress that the Hebrew construction cannot refer to the period from the destruction of Jerusalem by Nebuchadressar onwards but instead refers to the period which ended in the catastrophe of 587/86 BCE. So e.g. I. Rabinowitz, 'A Reconsideration of "Damascus" and "390 Years" in the "Damascus" ("Zadokite") Fragments', *JBL* 73 (1954), pp. 11-35, esp. 33-34; E. Wiesenberg, 'Chronological Data in the Zadokite Fragments', *VT* 5 (1955), pp. 284-308. This view is improbable, however. Even though I admit that there are some linguistic data which support the view, it can be rejected for contextual reasons. In CD I it is stressed that after the period of wrath God established the holy remnant of Israel, which after 20 years received from God the Teacher of Righteousness. If the 390-year period ended in 587/86 BCE, CD would suggest that the Teacher of Righteousness lived in the 6th century BCE, which is absurd. On the other hand, if the 390-year period is calculated as beginning from the year 587/86, then the appearance of the Teacher of Righteousness would be in the 2nd century BCE, which is plausible from an historical point of view.

The total length of these four epochs is 450 years + the length of the period of the activity of the Teacher of Righteousness. If this period is estimated to be 40 years, then we arrive at 490 years which agrees precisely with the figure given in Daniel 9. However, this connection between the chronological systems of the Damascus Document and Daniel 9 remains uncertain.

Perhaps it is more interesting to ponder how accurate the chronological system described in the Damascus Document is. The general trend among scholars has been to regard this system as unreliable. The argument is that the chronological data concerning the intertestamental period are very inaccurate in other sources e.g. Daniel, Josephus and Demetrius. Therefore, according to major scholars the chronology of the Damascus Document cannot be used to calculate a precise date for the birth of the Qumran community.[9]

The chronology of Demetrius provides us with a fresh backdrop for a reevaluation of the chronological system in the Damascus Document. It should be noted that we have no reason, *prima facie*, to assume that the chronological system of the Damascus Document is inaccurate simply because the chronological systems of the intertestamental period are incoherent. We can investigate the potential historical value of the chronology in the Damascus Document by tentatively assuming (1) that it is accurate; (2) that it is about 26/27 years shorter than the actual chronology of the period (such as Demetrius, who lived at the end of the 3rd century BCE).

1. By assuming that the figure 390 is accurate, we may fix this period of wrath to 586–197 BCE. This point in time in the history of Israel is of great interest. At about this time (201–198 BCE[10]) the Seleucids, under the leadership of Antiochus III, wrested Palestine from the Ptolemies. Josephus recounts that the Jews in Jerusalem were positively inclined toward Antiochus III. They joined up with him, gave plentiful provision to his army and assisted him in his siege of the Egyptian garrison in the citadel of Jerusalem. The king in turn reduced their taxes and did all he

---

9. See e.g. H.H. Rowley, *The Zadokite Fragments and the Dead Sea Scrolls* (Oxford: Blackwell, 1952), pp. 62-64; G. Vermes, *The Dead Sea Scrolls: Qumran in Perspective* (London: SCM Press, 1994), pp. 158-59; F.M. Cross, *The Ancient Library of Qumran* (Sheffield: Sheffield Academic Press, 1995), pp. 100-101; P. Davies, *The Damascus Covenant. An Interpretation of the 'Damascus Covenant'* (JSOTSup, 25; Sheffield: Sheffield Academic Press, 1983), pp. 67, 199; P.R. Callaway, *The History of the Qumran Community: An Investigation* (JSPSup, 3; Sheffield: Sheffield Academic Press, 1988), pp. 127-31.

10. The decisive battle was at Panion in 198 BCE.

could to 'requite the zeal and exertions of the Jews' (*Ant.* 12.134). This account only presents a half-truth, however. In Dan. 11.13-14 those Jews who were positively inclined toward Antiochus are accused of being 'the violent men' who, by supporting Antiochus, have tried 'to accomplish a vision, but they will stumble' (v. 14). The reference here is probably to the fact that some Jews tried to release their country entirely from the yoke of foreign oppression – the hope held out in so many prophetic passages – but had no success in their endeavors.[11] It is a plausible assumption that some Jews regarded the imposition of the yoke of the Seleucids as a decisively negative turning point in the history of the people. They could have formed a religious group which was only loosely organized until more organization was provided under the leadership of the Teacher of Righteousness (cf. CD I, 9-10).

Fixing the date of the birth of the community to the beginning of the Seleucid period entails that the Teacher of Righteousness began his activity in about 175 BCE, which corresponds with the accession year of Antiochus IV Epiphanes. This synchronism also fits in well with the important historical events of the time. We may suppose that the character of Antiochus' religious policy forced the organization of the community (to be subsumed) under the leadership of the Teacher of Righteousness. He was apparently a fanatic adherent of the Jewish religion and therefore could not follow the syncretistic religious policy of Antiochus.

2. If, however, the chronological system of CD, like that of Demetrius, differs from that of the actual chronology by 26/27 years, then the 'period of wrath' refers to the years 586–170 BCE and the appearance of the Teacher of Righteousness would have taken place in about 150 BCE. These dates harmonize well with the events in the history of the Jewish people. The birth of the community would thus be contemporaneous with the events in Jerusalem around 170 BCE, when Onias III was murdered and a syncretistic religious program was promulgated there. The appearance of the Teacher of Righteousness would be contemporaneous with the conflict which arose when the Hasmonean dynasty began to assert itself not only in the political but also in the religious life of Judah.

Which of the two alternatives is more probable? For an answer to this question, we must turn to the content of the Qumran scrolls. It seems reasonable to assume on the basis of their content that a conflict arose between the Qumran community and the Hasmonean dynasty, which held

---

11. See A. Lacocque, *The Book of Daniel* (London: SPCK, 1979), p. 224; cf. also J.J. Collins, *Daniel: A Commentary on the Book of Daniel* (Hermeneia; Minneapolis: Fortress Press, 1993), pp. 379-80.

the High Priest's office from the time of Jonathan Maccabeus onwards. It is clear that the Hasmoneans were regarded as illegitimate High Priests (cf. 1QpHab VIII, 16f; IX, 1-7). Against this background the second alternative above seems to be the more probable.[12] In addition, if we assume that the date of the appearance of the Teacher of Righteousness is about 150 BCE then 'the wicked priest' mentioned in Qumran scrolls must refer to Jonathan (so Vermes) and not to Simon (so Cross).[13]

The conclusion is that there is a good deal of evidence which speaks for the fact that the writer of CD has intentionally tried to place the birth of the community within the chronology of the history of Israel with which he was familiar. In any case the chronological system used in CD seems to be in harmony with that used by the Jewish historiographer, Demetrius, in the 3rd century BCE.

In order to demonstrate how Demetrius's chronological system *de facto* explains well the early Jewish chronological speculations we shall still take one example from the Syriac Baruch or Second Baruch.

The Chronology in Second Baruch

It is a generally accepted view that the Apocalypse of the Syriac Baruch (= *2 Baruch*) was written between the destruction of the Second Temple and the Bar Kochba war. The *terminus ad quem* is established by a reference in the *Epistle of Barnabas* (*Ep. Barn.*) to 2 Baruch: *Ep. Barn.* 11.9 quotes *2 Bar.* 61.7.[14] On the other hand, *Ep. Barn.* 16.4 indicates that a pagan temple was being built in Jerusalem. This description may refer to 117 CE or 132 CE, indicating that the *terminus ad quem* should be fixed during the Bar Kochba war.[15]

---

12. It is worth noting, however, that 1QpHab presupposes that 'the wicked priest' rejected the message of the Teacher of Righteousness – something which may indicate that the latter had acted before the former had assumed the office of High Priest. Unfortunately the scrolls do not mention how long the Teacher of Righteousness acted as leader of the community. If his period of activity lasted about 40 years (see above!), then the first alternative cannot be categorically rejected, i.e. that the Teacher of Righteousness began to act about 175 BCE and died about 135 BCE.

13. See these interpretations in Vermes, *The Dead Sea Scrolls*; Cross, *The Ancient Library of Qumran*; T. Lim, 'Wicked Priest', in L.H. Schiffman and J.C. VanderKam (eds.), *Encyclopedia of the Dead Sea Scrolls*, I–II (Oxford: Oxford University Press, 2000), II, pp. 973-76.

14. One may ask whether *Ep. Barn.* 11.9 really quotes *2 Bar.* 61.7 or whether it is an imprecise allusion to Zeph. 3.19. In any case there is good historical reason to argue that *2 Baruch* (like *4 Ezra*) is composed before the Bar Kochba war.

15. Concerning this date see A. F. J. Klijn translation and comments for 2 Baruch in *OTP*, I, pp. 616-17.

N. Roddy has proposed a date for 2 Baruch on the basis of statements made in *2 Bar.* 28.2: 'For the measure and the calculation of that time will be two parts: weeks of seven weeks (*trtyn mnwn šbw' 'dšb'' šbw'yn*)'.[16] He criticizes Klijn's view that this passage cannot be used to date the work.[17] Roddy argues that the number in *2 Bar.* 28.2 should be interpreted as $2 \times (7 \times 7^2) = 686$ years which implies that, according to the author, the end would have come in 99 CE (i.e., 587 BCE + 686 years = 99 CE). Thus the *terminus ad quem* for the composition of the work would be 99 CE.[18] Roddy's date is problematic at two points, however. He has overlooked the fact that the chronological systems of ancient texts do not correspond precisely to modern dating systems. We have seen how the 70 yearweeks in Dan. 9.24-27 have been used to create the chronological system of the postexilic period in Josephus's writings. Demetrius chronology is another indication that the postexilic Jewish chronology was not accurate. Therefore, we may presuppose that the author of Second Baruch was familiar with some ancient inaccurate chronological system.

Another weakness is that it is not clear which date represents the starting point from which the 686 years should be calculated. According to Roddy, the number 686 should be calculated from 587 BCE. However, the opening verse in 2 Baruch indicates that Baruch received his vision in the 25th year of Jeconiah. This date is important because it stands in tension with 2 Baruch 8's statements that Zedekiah was captured by Nebuchadrezzar. This event took place before the 25th year of Jeconiah. According to Klijn, this discrepancy is due to inaccuracy on the author's part.[19] However, this solution cannot explain the author's reasons for dating this apocalyptic vision to the 25th year of Jeconiah. It seems to me that the 25th year of Jeconiah is fabricated in order to convey information to the reader concerning the end. I propose that the 686 years should be calculated from the 25th year of Jeconiah and not from the fall of Jerusalem. Assuming that the chronological system which the author of 2 Baruch knew differed from the modern dating system, we may test two options: the chronology of Josephus and that of Demetrius.

According to the first option, the time span between the destruction of the First and the Second Temple would be 639 (= the time between the return and the destruction of the Second Temple according to *Bell. Jud.* 6.270) + 70 (the length of the exile, *Ant.* 11.1) = 709 years.

16. N. Roddy, ' "Two Parts: Weeks of Seven Weeks": The End of the Age as *Terminus ad Quem* for *2 Baruch*', *JSP* 14 (1996), pp. 3-14.
17. See Klijn's view in *The Old Testament Pseudepigrapha*, I, pp. 616-17.
18. Roddy, 'Two Parts: Weeks of Seven Weeks', pp. 11-14.
19. See *Old Testament Pseudepigrapha*, I, p. 621 n. 1a.

The period from the 25th year of Jeconiah and the destruction of the Second Temple would be 709 – 14 = 695 years. This reasoning would mean that the end would have come, according to the author about nine years (695 – 686 = 9) before the destruction of the Second Temple which is absolutely impossible. On the other hand, we have no reason to suppose that the author of 2 Baruch would have been an adherent of Josephus's ideological history. Josephus represented a peaceful and pro-Roman ideology while the author of 2 Baruch regarded the Roman Empire as an evil kingdom.[20] Given these orientations, we have reason to believe that the chronological system adopted by the author of 2 Baruch was not that of Josephus. We have already argued that the chronological system in the Damascus Document may follow the chronology of Demetrius. If this is true, then the establishment of the Qumran community would have taken place in 151 BCE, which is reconcilable with what we know of the historical circumstances of the Hasmonean period. At that time Jonathan was appointed as High Priest in Jerusalem and the establishment of the Qumran community was probably a protest against this event.[21]

Assuming that the author followed the dating system of Demetrius (known to Clement of Alexandria) his chronological system was 26 years shorter than the actual chronology. Thus, the period from the 25th year of Jeconiah to the destruction of the Second Temple would be 587 + 70 – 26 – 14 = 617 years. This calculation implies that, according to the author of 2 Baruch, the end would come about 69 years after the destruction of the Second Temple, i.e., in 139 CE. This hypothesis might provide a sound explanation for the Bar Kochba war beginning in 132 CE. The war was an attempt to actualize the apocalyptic chronology. According to the book of Jeremiah, the First Temple was to be rebuilt after 70 years' captivity. It was believed that the same would apply to the Second Temple. This being the case, the Third Temple was expected to be rebuilt around 139/140 CE. On the other hand, in Dan. 9.24-27 the end is preceded by seven years of war – which means that the decisive final battle would begin around 132/133 CE. In 2 Baruch the mystical number 686 was calculated so that the balance between the destruction of the First and the Second Temple as well as their rebuildings would correspond to the predictions in the Books of Jeremiah and Daniel. Bar Kochba began the bloody battle against Rome about seven years before the time appointed for the rebuilding of the Third Temple in Jerusalem.

20. Rome is the fourth evil kingdom in *2 Bar.* 39–40.
21. See A. Laato, 'The Chronology of the Damascus Document of Qumran', *RQ* 60 (1992), pp. 605-607.

Coins from the time of this revolt clearly indicate the aim of Bar Kochba: the liberation of Zion.[22] If our interpretation is correct then the apocalyptic numbers in 2 Baruch refer to the crisis documented in later Rabbinical writings in a literary context in which the war of Bar Kochba is also referred to (see, e.g., the Babylonian Talmud, *Sanhedrin* 96b-97b, 99a): It is not possible to calculate the time of the end, only God knows.[23] The author of 2 Baruch was sure that his apocalyptic calculations had revealed to him the mystery which allowed him to arrive at the conclusion that the rebuilding of the new Jerusalem and the Temple (*2 Bar.* 4) would be realized in the near future.

Our investigation to this point suggests that there was an inaccuracy of 26/27 years in postexilic Jewish chronology. One possible way of explaining the outcome of this inaccuracy is that the actual length of the exile was 49 years, while in Jewish chronological tradition the 70-year exile predicted by Jeremiah was adopted. In that way we have possibility to decrease the inaccuracy to only to 5/6 years.

We have seen that there were two fundamentally different chronological systems in early Jewish writings: Josephus based his chronology on Dan. 9.24-27 and regarded the seventy yearweeks as corresponding accurately to the period between the destruction of the First Temple and the Maccabean period. Demetrius represented another chronological system which was probably followed in the Damascus Document and the Syriac Baruch Apocalypse. But how can we explain the outcome of the chronological system in Dan. 9.24-27? This is now our next task.

The Outcome of the Chronological System in Daniel 9.24-27

Dan. 9.24-27 has been one of the most difficult passages to interpret in the book of Daniel.[24] Already in 1927 Montgomery wrote concerning this passage as follows: 'The history of the exegesis of the 70 Weeks is the Dismal Swamp of O.T. criticism'.[25] A similar utterance can be found from Koch's survey of research on the book of Daniel: 'In der

22. See the coins in Y. Yadin, *Bar-Kokhba: The Rediscovery of the Legendary Hero of the Last Jewish Revolt against Imperial Rome* (London: Weidenfeld & Nicolson, 1971).
23. For the interpretation of this Talmudic passage see J. Neusner, *Messiah in Context: Israel's History and Destiny in Formative Judaism* (Philadelphia: Fortress Press, 1984), pp. 168-78.
24. See Collins, *Daniel*, pp. 352-58.
25. Montgomery, *Book of Daniel*, p. 400. This opinion has also been quoted in T.E. McComiskey, 'The Seventy "Weeks" of Daniel against the Background of Ancient Near Eastern Literature', *WTJ* 47 (1985), pp. 18-45, esp. 18.

Geschichte der Danielexegese ist kein anderer Abschnitt so eingehend und so kontrovers behandelt worden wie dieser'.[26] The difficulty in getting the length of the second apocalyptical epoch to fit in between the return from the Exile and the Maccabean period is mainly solved among scholars by referring to the fact that chronological data about the intertestamental period in the book of Daniel as well as in other sources are inexact. Reference is made to the following:

1. The chronological data in the book of Daniel can be very inaccurate as can be seen from Dan. 11.2. According to that verse, there would have been only four kings in the Persian Empire before the Macedonian conquest – all ancient and modern interpreters agree that Dan. 11.4 refers to Alexander the Great. Such chronological information has been regarded as a proof that the author(s) of the book of Daniel had no real knowledge of Persian history. This view, then, has been related to the chronological data in Dan. 9.24-27, which in a similar way gives us historically inaccurate information.[27]

2. Further, as already noted scholars often refer to Schürer's remark, according to which both Josephus and the Hellenistic Jewish historiographer Demetrius (from the end of the third century BCE) have the corresponding inaccuracy in their chronology of the intertestamental period.[28]

3. The 70 yearweeks are connected with the prophecy of Jeremiah (25.11-12; 29.10) that the Exile will endure for 70 years and the data in 2 Chron. 36.21, according to which the return from the Exile will be realized only when 'the country has paid off his Sabbaths'. These biblical passages have implied the idea of 70 yearweeks, which does not inevitably refer to the real chronology.[29]

4. Koch has put forward the argument that the 490 years' period is connected with the chronological data given in the Deuteronomistic historiography. According to it, there were 480 years between the Exodus from Egypt and the beginning of the building of the First Temple in Solomon's fourth year (1 Kgs 6.1). The sum of the regnal years of the Judean kings from that time to the Babylonian Exile is 430 years. When these two

26. K. Koch, *Das Buch Daniel* (EdF, 144; Darmstadt: Wissenschaftliche Buchgesellschaft, 1980), p. 149.
27. So Koch, *Daniel*, p. 152.
28. Schürer, *Geschichte de jüdischen Volkes*, pp. 266-67.
29. So e.g. Porteous, *Danielbuch*, pp. 17-18.

figures are calculated and the 70 years of Exile are added to it, as prophesied by Jeremiah (Jer. 25.11-12; 29.10), we get 980 years, which is twice 490 years.[30]

As far as point (1) is concerned, it is hardly possible to regard the author of the book of Daniel as so lacking in knowledge about the Persian period that he really imagined that there were only four Persian kings.[31] In that case the writer of the book of Daniel would have radically shortened the chronology between the exile and the Maccabean period, but Dan. 9.24-27 is evidence for the contrary. Therefore, we can suppose that he knew that the Persian period lasted for about 200 years. But how can we, in this case, explain the passage in Dan. 11.2-4? I propose the following interpretation. Behind Dan. 11.2-4 looms an old prophetic-eschatological or apocalyptic tradition, according to which Persia would be annihilated by the Greeks (= Javan). This tradition originates from the beginning of the Persian period, from the time of the Persian wars. This view actually receives support from the text. In Dan. 11.2 it is stressed how Persia tries to destroy Javan. This statement does not correspond to the historical situation at the end of the fourth century, as during that period it was Javan that was active against Persia. On the other hand, Dan. 11.2 fits in well with the historical situation at the beginning of the fifth century when the Persians attacked the Greeks at Marathon (490 BCE), Thermopylai (489 BCE) and Salamis (480 BCE). If this assumption is right, then the four Persian kings mentioned in Dan. 11.2 are Cyrus, Cambyses, Dareios I (522–486) and Xerxes I (486–465). The attributes of the fourth king of Persia in particular fit in well with Xerxes I, who was known for his hostility against the Greeks and for his wealth.[32] On the other hand, Dareios III, who was defeated by Alexander, cannot be characterized with the words used in Dan. 11.2.[33] This being the case,

---

30. See K. Koch, 'Die mysteriösen Zahlen der judäischen Könige und die apokalyptischen Jahrwochen', *VT* 28 (1978), pp. 433-41.

31. Collins (*Daniel*, 377) writes that 'the passage reflects a drastically abbreviated history of the Persian Empire'. He continues that the fourth king was 'then most plausibly the last Persian king, Darius III Codomannus'. Apparently, the author of the present form of the book of Daniel had Darius III in his mind.

32. The Hebrew text at the end of Dan. 11.2 is not very clear: 'he will stir up everything, the kingdom of Greek'. However, early Greek versions have understood the passage so that the Persian king will attack against the kingdom of Greece. See Collins, *Daniel*, p. 363. Such an interpretation is clearly plausible to the Hebrew text. Concerning the aggression of Xerxes I against Greece, see, e.g., B. Reicke, *Neutestamentliche Zeitgeschichte. Die biblische Welt von 500 v.Chr. bis 100 n.Chr* (Dritte verbesserte Auflage; Berlin: W. de Gruyter, 1982), p. 13.

33. Cf. Reicke, *Neutestamentliche Zeitgeschichte*, p. 30.

Dan. 11.2-4 is based on an older tradition from the time of the Persian wars when a Judean apocalyptic group expected the Persians to be defeated by the Greeks and that Judea would be set free from Persian occupation. The struggles in Greece during early 5th century BCE when the Persian troops were defeated created such expectations among Judeans. This tradition was then reformulated in its present form to suit the context of Daniel 10–12 better.[34] In conclusion, we can note that Dan. 11.2 cannot be used as an argument that the author of the book of Daniel was so unfamiliar with the past history of Israel that he could not therefore give us any more accurate chronology than that in Dan. 9.24-27.

Point (2) cannot explain the inaccuracy in the chronological data of Dan. 9.24-27 either. We have seen that Josephus's chronology is simply based on Dan. 9.24-27 and Schürer's argument is circular. Demetrius's chronology in turn is much shorter than the actual chronology and provides no parallel to Dan. 9.24-27.

More promising therefore, is the interpretive model which is based on points 3 and 4. That the seventy years' exile plays an important role in the book of Daniel is clear from Dan. 1.1-2 and 9.2.[35] As far as Dan. 1.1-2 is concerned, scholars have often proposed that the Judean exile in 606/605 BCE is created in order to make the prophecy of Jeremiah agree with reality. Indeed, there were about 70 years between 606/605 and 538/537 BCE.[36] In this case it is plausible to assume that the idea of the 70 yearweeks originates from the Chronicler's account in 2 Chron. 36.21.

Koch's solution is interesting, even though he has not explained why the 70 yearweeks have been divided as they are, and in particular there is no explanation from where the length of the second epoch is derived.

---

34. In this connection it is worth noticing that Josephus says that the prophecy transmitted in the name of Daniel, according to which Javan would defeat Persia, was shown to Alexander the Great when he came to Judea (*Ant.* XI, 337). Of course, the historicity of this story is not self-evident and could have been created by Josephus by way of an apology in order to legitimate his prophecy, according to which Vespasianus would become Caesar. But even though the story might have been used by Josephus as an apology, its historicity cannot be categorically denied. If there is some historical core in the story then Dan. 11.2 could have been a pre-Maccabean tradition from the beginning of the Persian period.

35. It is also worth noting that Darius was 62 years old when he became king (Dan. 6.1). This number may be symbolic and correspond to 62 yearweeks in Dan. 9.24-27. Concerning this see R. Kratz, 'The Visions of Daniel', in J.J. Collins and P.W. Flint (eds.), *The Book of Daniel: Composition and Reception*, I (VTSup, 83/1; Leiden: Brill, 2001), pp. 91-113, esp. 110.

36. So e.g. Montgomery, *Daniel*, pp. 113-17; Porteous, *Danielbuch*, pp. 17-18 and K. Koch, *Daniel* (BKAT, 22/1; Neukichen–Vluyn: Neukirchener Verlag, 1986), pp. 29-30.

Before presenting a new view of Dan. 9.24-27, I shall first make some observations on the text of Dan. 9.24-27. I translate the texts as following:[37]

24 Seventy weeks are decreed
    for your people and your holy city,
    for putting an end to transgression,
    for placing the seal on sin,
    for expiating crime,
    for introducing everlasting uprightness
    for setting the seal on vision and on prophecy,
    for anointing the holy of holies.
25 Know this, then, and understand:
    From the time there went out this message:
    'Return and rebuild Jerusalem'
    to the coming of an Anointed Prince,
    seven weeks and sixty-two weeks,
    with squares and ramparts
    restored and rebuilt,
    but in a time of trouble.
26 And after the sixty-two weeks
    Anointed One put to death and he is no longer[38]
    and city and sanctuary ruined
    by a prince who is to come.
    The end of that prince will be catastrophe
    and, until the end, there will be war
    and all the devastation decreed.
27 He will do the covenant heavy for the many
    for the space of a week;
    and for the space of one half-week
    he will put a stop to sacrifice and oblation,
    and with the wing of desolation he will come
    until the end, until the doom assigned to the devastator.

In the Maccabean context, the passage is best explained in such a way that the reference in v. 26 is made to the murder of Onias III recorded in 2 Macc. 4.23-28 (cf. Dan. 11.22). Verse 27 is also easily connected to

---

37. The translation is mainly based on the New Jerusalem Bible.
38. The Hebrew *'ên lô* is difficult to interpret. There are different possibilities (see Collins, *Daniel*, pp. 346, 356-57): (1) In the Septuagint, this expression has been translated: 'he is no longer'; (2) Theodotion translated 'there is no judgment'; (3) some scholars connect the phrase with the following word: 'the city was no longer for him' (e.g., L.F. Hartman and A. DiLella, *The Book of Daniel* [AB, 23; New York: Doubleday, 1978], p. 240); (4) Collins emendates the passage according to Dan. 11.45: 'No one to help him'.

the Maccabean period. P.L. Redditt has argued that Daniel 9 forms a coherent literary structure from the Maccabean time. It begins with a reference to 70 years' captivity and ends with an interpretation of this captivity in 70 yearweeks.[39]

As far as the literary character of Dan. 9.24-27 is concerned, there is a clear contrast between the information in v. 26, according to which the holy city and the temple will be ruined and that in v. 27, according to which the coming prince will put an end to sacrifice and oblation in the temple.[40] Thus in v. 27 it is assumed that the temple still exists, something which is in disharmony with v. 26. On the other hand, v. 27b is closely connected with the history of the Maccabean period and therefore we can assume that it is a Maccabean actualization in Dan. 9.24-27. The same can be said about 27a. Moreover, its content is closely connected with the persecutions during the Maccabean period. Also 27c can be regarded as a Maccabean actualization of Isa. 8.8b. Next we shall briefly discuss the traditio-historical background of vv. 24-26.

Scholars seem to agree today that the Anointed One refers to the High Priest. This view is probably right as far as the present context of Dan. 9.24-27 is concerned because the text was seen to speak about the murder of Onias III. The problem is, however, the word *nāgîd* in v. 25. Even though the Davidic dynasty was never reestablished after the exile, the Davidic princes played an important role at least at the beginning of the Persian period, as can be seen from the genealogy preserved in 1 Chron. 3.17-24.[41] Traditionally *nāgîd* and *māšîah* were the titles used for the kings even though they could also be used for High Priests.[42] If we assume that in Dan. 9.24-26 the words *nāgîd* and *māšîah* referred to a Davidic prince, how can we explain the origin of this kind of a tradition, according to which the Davidic prince will be killed in the final struggle? In order to answer this question we must first discuss the important traditio-historical motif in Dan. 9.24-26, namely 'Völkerkampf'.

---

39. P.L. Redditt, 'Daniel 9: Its Structure and Meaning', *CBQ* 62 (2000), pp. 236-49.

40. It is worth noting that many modern interpreters take the destruction of the city symbolically. For example, Collins (*Daniel*, p. 357) writes: 'The Syrians did not demolish Jerusalem, but they made it desolate by the corruption of the cult'. However, such an interpretation is possible in the light of v. 27. The literal meaning of v. 26 indicates the destruction of the city and the sanctuary.

41. Cf. P. Hanson, *Dawn of Apocalyptic* (Philadelphia: Fortress Press, 1975), pp. 348-49.

42. For *nāgîd* see, e.g., 1 Chron. 9.11, 20; 26.24; cf. also Jer. 20.1.

6. The Postbiblical Chronology

The 'Völkerkampf' is a central eschatological theme in the Hebrew Bible and its main motif is the nations attacking Zion. This theme is already apparent in the old Zion tradition, which may originate from the Jebusite Zion (cf. 2 Sam. 5.7-8). After the Exile this theme was further developed, as can be seen from texts such as Ezekiel 38–39; Joel 4; Zechariah 12 and 14. The central idea in Ezekiel 38–39 is that Yahweh himself provokes the attack of Goog and the other nations in Jerusalem, where the people who had returned from the Exile live unprotected – but who, however, enjoyed Yahweh's protection (see Ezek. 38.4, 11). The aim of Yahweh is to show to the nations that the Israelites were not deported into exile because their God was unable to prevent it (cf. Ezek. 38.23) but because they had sinned against their God (Ezek. 39.23). By doing this Yahweh would cleanse his name which was defiled by the Israelites among the nations (see especially Ezek. 36.20-32). Yahweh provokes this war in order to reverse the events of the year 586 BCE. The nations will try to annihilate the people who live without walls but Yahweh shows his great might to all peoples by redeeming his people and destroying the attacking nations. The same provocation motif is also visible in Joel 4 (see especially v. 2), which mainly follows the order of events in Ezekiel 38–39. In Zechariah 12 and 14 the idea has been developed further. In Zechariah 14 the nations are allowed to attack and destroy Jerusalem while God makes a refuge for his people through the Mount of Olives (Zech. 14.2-4). In this sense Zechariah 14 is quite reminiscent of the corresponding theme in Dan. 9.24-26, where the attacker also destroys Jerusalem but cannot annihilate the people. In Zechariah 12 the ideas of the attacking nations and the death of the Messiah are connected with each other so that the inhabitants of Jerusalem and the members of the Davidic House mourn the death of the 'pierced one' (= Messiah, see vv. 10-13).[43] Both these ideas have been combined in Zech. 13.7-9: the death of the good shepherd (=Messiah)[44] is

---

43. In Zech. 12.11 Yahweh identifies himself with the good shepherd i.e. Messiah. See e.g. W. Rudolph, *Haggai – Sacharja 1–8 – Sacharja 9–14 – Maleachi* (KAT, 13/4; Gütersloh: Gütersloher Verlagshaus Mohn 1976), pp. 217-18; Laato, *Josiah and David Redivivus*, pp. 268-94; Laato, *A Star Is Rising*, pp. 208-18.

44. Some scholars stress that the death of the shepherd in 13.7 refers to the evil shepherd in 11.15-17. See e.g. B. Stade, 'Deuterozacharja. Eine kritische Studie', *ZAW* 1 (1881), pp. 1-96, esp. 29-32; W. Nowack's (*Die kleinen Propheten* [HAT. 3/4, 369; Göttingen: Vandenhoeck & Ruprecht, 1922], pp. 373-75), K. Marti's (*Das Dodekapropheton* [KH-CAT, 13/2; Tübingen: Mohr, 1904], pp. 442-43) and H.G. Mitchell's (*A Critical and Exegetical Commentary on Haggai and Zechariah* [ICC; Edinburgh: T. & T. Clark, 1912], pp. 314-19) commentaries; J. Wellhausen, *Die kleine Propheten übersetzt und erklärt* (Berlin: W. de Gruyter, 1963), pp. 192-96.

followed by the purification operation which finally will lead to the birth of a new people. In Dan. 9.24-26 this idea is developed further. The Messiah will be killed in the final struggle, which will last seven years.

The pre-Maccabean tradition of the apocalyptical yearweeks in Dan. 9.24-27 also contained three epochs:

1. 7 yearweeks – from the exile to the return
2. 62 yearweeks – rebuilding of Jerusalem
3. 1 yearweek – the final struggle

That the 7 yearweeks refer to the years 586–538/7 BCE is clear. As far as the 62 yearweeks are concerned, they seem to be connected with the regnal years of the Judean kings from Solomon to Zedekiah, which total 434 years.[45] This epoch may be interpreted so that the people must live righteously according to the commandments of Yahweh for as many years as the Davidic kings after David reigned in Judah and during which the commandments of Yahweh had not been obeyed. When this epoch ends, Yahweh will bring upon the people distress resembling that of the year 586 BCE, the final result of which is, however, victory for Israel. During the seven years' hard struggle Israel will finally be victorious – but at great cost (Jerusalem and the temple will be ruined; cf. Zech. 14) and the Davidic (alternatively Aaronite) *māšiaḥ* will be killed (cf. Zech. 12). Probably this final struggle must be understood as some kind of purification operation as in Zech. 13.7-9, where those among the people who have not lived according to Yahweh's commandments will be killed and those who have been loyal to Yahweh will be saved. In any case it seems to be clear that after this struggle there will be a new marvelous time for the people of Israel.

By interpreting Dan. 9.24-26 in the light of Zechariah 12–14 there is no need to take the Maccabean period as the origin apocalyptical epochs of the seventy yearweeks. In this new solution it also becomes clear why the apocalyptical epochs have been divided in the way they have been. The first epoch stems from historical reality i.e. from the length of the Exile. The second epoch was derived from the chronology of the Deuteronomistic historiography. The remaining seven years is interpreted as referring to the length of the final struggle. This apocalyptical

---

(See also 'The New English Bible' where 13.7-9 is added after 11.17.) Rudolph has rejected this interpretation by noting rightly that the evil shepherd could hardly be called by Yahweh as 'my shepherd' or as one 'who works with me'. On the other hand, these characterizations fit in well with the good shepherd with whom Yahweh identifies himself in Zech 11.4-14. See Rudolph (*Haggai – Sacharja*, pp. 213-15).

45. Cf. Koch, 'Die mysteriösen Zahlen', p. 435.

theme was then actualized during the Maccabean period. At that time the murder of Onias III was seen as fulfilling the utterance of the death of *nāgîd*, and *māšîaḥ* was interpreted as referring to Onias III. It was believed that the 62 yearweeks were fulfilled (which they were not in reality) and the last struggle would soon begin. It was in this apocalyptical atmosphere that the Maccabeans began their revolt against Antiochus in the belief that the Kingdom of God would soon come to them.

7

THE DEUTERONOMISTIC CHRONOLOGICAL FRAMEWORK FOR EARLY ISRAEL

We have seen how the biblical postexilic and later Jewish chronological traditions contained inaccuracies which led to many decades' difference in the chronological systems of Jewish chronographers. The reason for this outcome was that unlike during the monarchic period there was no official recording system to calculate years in the postexilic times and later. In a similar way we may expect that attempts to present premonarchic chronology in the biblical sources are not based on any real historical figures. Our main question in this Chapter 7 is whether we can argue that during the exilic period, the biblical writers adopted an older chronological tradition when they presented events in pre-monarchic times.

The Hebrew Bible contains five longer epochs of time which are as follows:

1. 400 years of slavery in Egypt (Gen. 15.13; cf. the fourth generation in Gen. 15.16). On the other hand, Exod. 12.40 indicates that Israelites were in Egypt for 430 years.
2. A 300-year period between the time of Jephthah and the occupation of Heshbon, Aroer and Arnon (Judg. 11.26).
3. 480 years between exodus from Egypt and the building of the Temple in the fourth regnal year of Solomon (1 Kgs 6.1)
4. The 70-year exile (Jer. 25.1-14)
5. 490 years between the events around the exile and the Maccabean times (Dan. 9.24-27)

From the lengths of the reigns of the Judean kings we can calculate that the period of the First Temple was 430 years because the sum of all Judean kings was 434 years and Solomon began to build the first temple in his 4th regnal year.[1] So we receive the following chronological scheme:

---

1. This idea goes back to J. Wellhausen, *Prolegomena zur Geschichte Israels* (Berlin: W. de Gruyter, 1927), pp. 270-71.

7. The Deuteronomistic Chronological Framework

Jacob's family living in Egypt
400 or 430 years
Exodus from Egypt
480 years
Solomon 4
430 years

Exile to Babylonia	Exile	Exile
	70 years' captivity	49 years' captivity
490 years	Return	
	420 years	434 years
Maccabean time	Maccabean time	7-year struggle Maccabean time

Galil has recently argued that according to the Deuteronomist, the period from the establishment of the First Temple until to its destruction lasted 400 years.[2] Galil calculates these 400 years in three different steps. The first step is from the destruction of the Temple to the destruction of Samaria according to the regnal years of the Judean kings i.e. 134 years. The second step is the period from the destruction of Samaria to the revolt of Judah according to the regnal years of the Israelite kings which lasted for 140 years. It is clear that the same period using the lengths of the reigns of the Judean kings would result in a different sum as can easily be seen from Table 4 given on p. 442 of Galil's article. The last step is the period from Jehu to the schism after the death of Solomon which lasted for about 90 years. This being the case, Galil's proposal presupposes a certain kind of artificial calculation by using the reigns of some Judean kings and the reigns of some Israelite kings. Galil's proposal is not valid however, as we use only the reigns of the Judean kings – something which Wellhausen emphasized in his proposal that the First Temple period according to the Deuteronomistic view lasted for 430 years. There are two additional arguments which support Wellhausen's viewpoint. First of all the figure 430 years in Exod. 12.40 supports the idea that the historical periods were divided to 430 (Israelites in Egypt), 480 (from the exodus to the establishment of the Temple) and 430 (the First Temple period) years. Secondly, we have seen that the seventy yearweeks were calculated according to the lengths of the reigns of the Judean kings from Solomon to Zedekiah (434 years = 62 yearweeks) and it is an additional argument that Wellhausen's proposal is valid.

---

2. Galil, 'Dates and Calendars'.

The period of 480 years in 1 Kgs 6.1 should be examined more closely. Was that period an idea which the Deuteronomist created in his historical work or could he have received it from an earlier tradition? In order to take stand on this matter we must examine all chronological details which the Deuteronomist gives us for the period between the exodus and the temple.

Joshua 5.6 and many chronological details in the Pentateuch indicate that the Israelites wandered in the desert for 40 years. Joshua 14.10-11 refers to Caleb being 85 years old when Joshua gave him land in the area of Judah (NIV): "Now then, just as the Lord promised, he has kept me alive for forty-five years since the time he said this to Moses, while Israel moved about in the wilderness. So here I am today, eighty-five years old! I am still as strong today as the day Moses sent me out; I am just as vigorous to go out to battle now as I was then." According to Num. 13.26-27 Caleb was 40 years of age when he was sent out as one of the spies into the land of Canaan (Num. 13.26-27). Numbers 10.11 indicates that the people left Sinai in the *second* year and the spies were apparently sent in the same year. This indicates that the event told in Josh 14.6-15 took place 6 years after the Israelites had come to the Land of Canaan. Thus Caleb was 40 + 39 = 79 years old when he came to the land of Canaan. There are no more chronological details in the Book of Joshua, but the Book of Judges contains a detailed chronological framework. I have listed the events and chronological details in the following table:

Judg. 3.8	Cushan-Rishathaim king of Aram Naharaim oppressed Israel for 8 years.
Judg. 3.11	Othniel saved Israel. Peace in Israel for 40 years.
Judg. 3.14	Eglon king of Moab subjugated Israel for 18 years.
Judg. 3.30	Ehud saved Israel. Peace for 80 years.
Judg. 4.3	Israel was under Jabin's and Sisera's rulership for 20 years.
Judg. 5.31	The victory of Barak and Debora led to peace in Israel for 40 years.
Judg. 6.1	Midianites oppressed Israel for 7 years.
Judg. 8.28	Gideon released Israel from the hands of Midianites; 40 years of peace.
Judg. 9.22	Abimelech was dictator in Shechem for 3 years.[3]
Judg. 10.2	Tola judged Israel for 23 years.
Judg. 10.3	Jair judged Israel for 22 years.[4]

---

3. It is possible that the three-year rule of Abimelech was part of the 40 years of peace mentioned in Judg. 8.28.
4. Tola and Jair are mentioned here in parallel. One may ask whether in older tradition these two judges were contemporaries, Tola in Israel (West from Jordan)

Judg. 10.8	Philistines and Ammonites oppressed Israel for 18 years.
Judg. 11.26	Israel has occupied Heshbon, Aroer and Arnon for 300 years
Judg. 12.7	Jephthah judged Israel for 6 years.
Judg. 12.9	Ibzan judged Israel for 7 years.
Judg. 12.11	Elon judged Israel for 10 years.
Judg. 12.14	Abdon judged Israel for 8 years.
Judg. 13.1	Philistines oppressed Israel for 40 years.
Judg. 15.20	Samson led Israel for 20 years in the days of the Philistines (cf. Judg. 16.31).[5]
1 Sam. 4.18	Eli led Israel for 40 years.

Judges 11.26 indicates that there were 300 years between the time of Jephthah and the settlement of the Trans-Jordan. However, when all the years from Cushan-Rishataim to Jephthah beginning with the six years' settlement in the land of Canaan are calculated we receive 6 + 8 + 40 + 18 + 80 + 20 + 40 + 7 + 40 + 3 + 23 + 22 + 18 = 325 years. The question is whether we should take the figure of 300 years in Jephthah's speech as an approximation and correspond it to these 325 years. However, there is another more challenging possibility, namely to regard the three-year rule of Abimelech as part of the 40 years of peace mentioned in Judg. 8.28, and thus regard Tola and Jair as contemporary judges in Israel and Gilead respectively. In that case we have exactly 300 years (= 6 + 8 + 40 + 18 + 80 + 20 + 40 + 7 + 40 + 23 + 18). This would imply that the chronological framework in Judges was pre-Deuteronomistic. It was the Deuteronomist who put Tola and Jair after each other, and Abimelech after 40 years of peace.

In the light of the chronological details which have been presented in the Deuteronomistic History the synchronism in 1 Kgs 6.1 becomes problematic because it states that the Temple was begun to be build 480 years after the Israelites left Egypt. All the chronological periods of the Judges together are 390 years (if Samson's 20 years are included in the 40 years of pressure by the Philistines). To this sum we must add both the 40 years of Eli (1 Sam. 4.18) and the 40 years of David (2 Sam. 5.4-5). In addition, the Israelite settlement in Canaan took at least 6 years as noted above and the building of the Temple was begun in Solomon's 4th regnal year. When we add these 90 years to 390 we already receive 480 years. In addition, between Eli and David we must calculate at least the

---

and Jair in Gilead (East of Jordan). In that case Jair's 22 years should be included in Tola's 23 years.

5. Judg. 15.20 apparently means that Samson led Israelites during the 40 years when the Philistines oppressed them.

periods of Samuel (not given) and Saul (at least 2 years; 1 Sam. 13.1;[6] cf. Acts 13.21: 40 years), and add the 40 years of wandering in the desert. This being the case we receive a substantially longer period than 480 years – the figure given in 1 Kgs 6.1.

We have seen that chronological details in the books of Joshua, Judges and Samuel indicate that the figure of 480 years in 1 Kgs 6.1 cannot be put in harmony with the Deuteronomistic chronology. If this is so we have reason to conclude that the Deuteronomist did not invent the figure in 1 Kgs 6.1, but rather he received it in tradition. This option receives support from the date in the verse, because it states that 'in the month of Ziv, the second month, he [Solomon] began to build the temple of Yahweh'. It seems that 'the month of Ziv' must be an earlier tradition which the Deuteronomist has commented on as 'the second month'. Therefore even the 480 years may be an older tradition. Do we have any possibility to reconstruct the details of this 480-years tradition? I think we have. It seems to me that we can combine the 300 year period mentioned in Judg. 11.26 to this 480-year period. Let me present arguments for this view.

The tradition in Josh. 14.6-15 emphasizes that Caleb was still strong and vigorous enough to go out to battle (vv. 10-11). However, according to the present form of the text Caleb would have been 85 years old. Apparently the text emphasizes ("miraculously") that 85-year old Caleb still was strong enough to battle against enemies of Israel. But the difficulty of regarding an 85-year-old man as a strong soldier opens up the possibility that there is an older tradition behind the text which emphasized the age of Caleb in another way. We may assume that the length of the period of wandering in the desert – taken as 40 years – was another chronological tradition which the Deuteronomist knew and integrated into his story. The Deuteronomist may have known another version of the exodus tradition which was related to the chronological system which he used in the Book of Judges, and in that tradition the length of the wandering from Egypt to Canaan was a much shorter period. This shorter period of wandering would correspond to the positive version of the exodus tradition which appears in Hos. 2.16-17; Jer. 2.2, 6 and Isaiah 40-55. If this is the case, then the older tradition behind Josh. 14.6-15 could have emphasized that Caleb was in his 40s. As noted already earlier it is possible to decrease the period of the Judges by 25 years, i.e. from 390 to 365 years. To this figure we must add the 40 years of Eli to

---

6. 1 Sam. 13.1 is a textually problematic passage and, for example, the Septuagint does not have any corresponding information about the length of the rule of Saul.

7. The Deuteronomistic Chronological Framework

the 40 years of David. Assuming that we have a 25-year period for Samuel and Saul (a figure not given in the Deuteronomistic History),[7] we receive the following epochs:

	6 years for exodus and settlement
	294 years to the time of Jephthah
	71 years from Jephthah to Eli
	40 years: Eli
	25 years: Samuel and Saul
	40 years: David
	4 years for Solomon
TOTAL:	480 years

This calculation implies that the figures of 480 years in 1 Kgs 6.1 and 300 years in Judg. 11.26 are part of pre-Deuteronomistic traditions. They contradict the present form of the Deuteronomistic chronology but enough material remains to present a hypothesis as to how these figures together provided a frame to present a coherent chronological system. Our result in this point is contrary to the way Hughes characterizes 1 Kgs 6.1: 'The figure of 480 years given in MT's text of 1 Kings 6.1 is typical of Priestly numerical schematism'.[8] We also disagree with him when he characterizes the figure of 300 years in Judg. 11.26: '... the figure of 300 years was inserted into its present context by the Deuteronomistic chronologist'.[9]

Historically seen, this 480-year period cannot be related to the absolute chronology. It is a well-known fact that the historical period in Canaan during the 1300s is well documented by the Amarna Letters which indicate that the Israelites were not yet in the land. It is therefore possible to date the exodus from Egypt only to the 13th century BCE. This fact implies that the biblical chronology in the pre-monarchic time cannot be regarded as historically reliable, and it is impossible to build any historical conclusions on that material.

---

7. It is worth noting that the Jewish historiographer Eupolemus from the 2nd century BCE "knows" that Saul reigned for 21 years (*OTP*, II, p. 866) but he does not give the length of the judgeship of Samuel. According to Josephus, Saul reigned for 20 years. These figures are not in harmony with 1 Sam. 7.2, according to which "the ark remained at Kiriath Jearim twenty years." This figure in 1 Sam. 7.2 gives an indication of the length of the period of Samuel and Saul but does not give any precise figure for them.

8. Hughes, *Secrets of the Times*, pp. 32-33.

9. Hughes, *Secrets of the Times*, pp. 73-74.

On the other hand, the 480 years between the exodus and the beginning of the building project of the Temple during Solomon's 4th regnal year can also be understood in such a way that there were twelve generations between the exodus and this building project. The length of one generation could have been estimated as 40 years, as becomes clear from the exodus tradition where 40 years is needed for the disappearance of one generation. If behind the figure of 480 years stand the 12 generations between the exodus and the time of Solomon, then the Levitical genealogies transmitted in 1 Chronicles 6 could give support for the chronological framework. According to that genealogy we can calculate that there are 12 generations from Aron, who acted during the time of exodus, to Achimas, the son of Zadok. I have argued elsewhere that the Levitical genealogy in 1 Chronicles 6 may well originate from the pre-exilic period.[10] This being the case a tradition of 480 (= 12 × 40) years could have been generated in the pre-Deuteronomistic period.

In this connection it is worth noting that in fact, twelve generations would mean about 12 × 25 years i.e. 300 years. Such a period of time could be placed between the period of the exodus in the 13th century BCE and the building-project of Solomon in the 960s.[11] This being the case, there is a plausible option that 1 Kgs 6.1 and Judg. 11.26 are parts of an ancient chronological scheme which was used in pre-exilic royal archives to connect the past history of Israel (the exodus and the settlement) to the chronology of the monarchy.

These results imply interesting possibilities to discuss the historical sources of the Deuteronomist. As noted in Chapter 2, the Deuteronomist refers to several literary sources which he had known. An old and still actual redaction-critical question is what kind of version or sources the Deuteronomist had when he edited his historical work. These fresh viewpoints on 1 Kgs 6.1 and Judg. 11.26 open a new window for scholars to think about the possibility that there was a pre-exilic version of the Deuteronomistic History, which was subsequently reworked totally

---

10. The date of the genealogies is of course the matter of discussion. I have argued that this list can well be dated to the pre-exilic period. See A. Laato, 'The Levitical Genealogies in 1 Chr 6 and the Formation of the Levitical Ideology in Postexilic Judah', *JSOT* 62 (1994), pp. 77-99.

11. The possibility to date the exodus in the reign of Ramses II is a well-known option despite of the fact that there are several tradition-historical, redaction-critical and historical problems which concern this early period of Israel. See Malamat, *History of Biblical Israel*; J.K. Hoffmeier, *Israel in Egypt: The Evidence for the Authenticity of the Exodus Tradition* (Oxford: Oxford University Press 1996); Hoffmeier, *Ancient Israel in Sinai: The Evidence for the Authenticity of the Wilderness Tradition* (Oxford: Oxford University Press 2005).

during the time of the exile.[12] If this is the case then we may have a pre-Deuteronomistic chronological scheme for the period of settlement and Judges.[13] Even though this chronological system of 480 years cannot be regarded as a reliable basis to understand the history of Early Israel it nevertheless gives scholars new evidence that we have pre-exilic material about Early Israel in the Deuteronomistic History.

---

12. See, in particular, Halpern and Lemaire, "The Composition of Kings'.
13. Concerning this, note especially Y. Amit, *Judges: Introduction and Commentary* [Hebrew] (Mikar LeYisra'el, Tel Aviv: Am Oved, 1999), pp. 3-22, esp. 11-13; Amit, *The Book of Judges: The Art of Editing* (Leiden: Brill, 1999); Amit, *History and ideology: An Introduction to Historiography in the Hebrew Bible* (Sheffield: Sheffield Academic Press, 1999), pp. 34-41.

8

THE PRIESTLY CHRONOLOGICAL FRAMEWORK FROM ANNO MUNDI TO PATRIARCHS

We shall conclude this study by dealing with the chronological system which is presented in the Pentateuch. Scholars relate this system to the Priestly author because the chronological details in Gen. 5.1-28, 30-32; 7:6; 9.28-29 and 11.10-26, 32 are formally almost identical.[1]

Genesis 5.1-28 and 11.10-26 contain interesting text-critical variants. Numerical figures in the Masoretic text, the Septuagint and the Samaritan Pentateuch differ from each other significantly. These differences are presented in the following table so that the lifetime of each figure are given according to Anno Mundi (= AM).[2]

	MT	LXX	SP
Adam	1–930	1–930	1–930
Seth	130–1042	230–1142	130–1042
Enosh	235–1140	435–1340	235–1140
Kenan	325–1235	625–1535	325–1235
Mahalalel	395–1290	795–1690	395–1290
Jared	460–1422	960–1922	460–1307
Enoch	622–987	1122–1487	522–887
Methuselah[3]	87–1656	1287–2256	587–1307
Lamech	874–1651	1454–2207	654–1307

1. See e.g. C. Westermann, *A Continental Commentary: Genesis 1–11* (Minneapolis: Fortress Press, 1994), pp. 353-54.; so also Hughes, *Secrets of the Times*, p. 6.

2. See this list in Hughes, *Secrets of the Times*, p. 12. It is worth noting that in p. 7 Hughes gives wrong columns to LXX and SP (Samaritan Pentateuch).

3. It is worth noting that according to the MT Methuselah died just before the Flood, while the chronological details in the LXX state that Methuselah still lived when the Flood came upon the world. In the SP three individuals die in the same year as the Flood (1307 AM): Jared, Methuselah and Lamech. This evidence indicates that the MT tradition has been preserved best. The LXX is simply illogical because Methuselah was not in the Ark, and the SP has preserved a corrupted tradition which was modified so that no pre-diluvian person survived the Flood other than Noah and his family.

Noah	1056–2006	1642–2592	707–1657
Shem	1556–2156	2142–2742	1207–1807
The Flood	1656	2242	1307
Arpachshad[4]	1658–2096	2244–2809	1309–1747
Kenan[5]		2379–2839	
Shelah	1693–2126	2509–2969	1444–1877
Eber	1723–2187	2639–3143	1574–1978
Peleg	1757–1996	2773–3112	1708–1947
Reu	1787–2026	2903–3242	1838–2077
Serug	1819–2049	3035–3365	1970–2200
Nahor	1849–1997	3165–3373	2100–2248
Terah	1878–2083	3344–3479	2179–2324
Abraham	1948	3414	2249

Scholars agree that these differences between the MT, LXX and SP cannot be explained by unintentional errors in copying texts.[6] The best way to explain these changes in the LXX is to assume that in the translation process, the numbers were changed in order to put them in better harmony with Hellenistic chronographs. The Jewish chronology was integrated in the Hellenistic chronographs from 3rd century BCE onwards, especially to those of Manetho[7] and Berossus,[8] which implies

---

4. According to Gen. 11.10, Arpachshad was born two years after the Flood. On the other hand, the same verse states that Shem was 100 years old when his son was born. However, Gen. 5.32 gives us information that Noah was 500 years old when his three sons were born and Gen. 7.6; 9.28 again that Noah was 600 years old when the Flood came over the world. These chronological details indicate that Shem should have been 102 years old when his boy Arpachshad was born.

5. H.R. Jacobus ('The Curse of Cainan [Jub. 8.1-5]: Genealogies in Genesis 5 and Genesis 11 and a Mathematical Pattern', *JSP* 18 [2009], pp. 207-32) has tried to show that there is a mathematical model which shows that Kenan was present in the proto-Masoretic text. Unfortunately her mathematical model is simplistic way to calculate $X1 + X2 + ...X10 - (X1 + X2 + ...X9) = X10$. This being the case the IA Difference in Genesis 5 is *de facto* the age of Noah after the birth of Shem (950–500 = 450) and RA difference in Gen. 5 is the age of Noah when Shem was born.

6. See e.g. R.W. Klein, 'Archaic Chronologies and the Textual History of the Old Testament', *HTR* 67 (1974), pp. 255-63; G. Larsson, 'The Chronology of the Pentateuch: A Comparison of the MT and LXX', *JBL* 102 (1983), pp. 401-409; Hughes, *Secrets of the Times*, pp. 5-30.

7. All available fragments of Manetho have been collected in W.G. Waddell, *Manetho* (LCL, 350; Cambridge, MA: Harvard University Press, 1980).

8. It can be shown that the so-called Pseudo-Eupolemus (preserved in Eusebius's *Praeparatio evangelica* 9.17.2-9) knew Berossus and integrated biblical history with the Babylonian historical version. See *JSHRZ* I:2, pp. 137-43; *OTP*, II, pp. 873-82; and B.Z. Wacholder, 'Pseudo-Eupolemus' Two Greek Fragments on the Life of Abraham', *HUCA* 34 (1963), pp. 83-113.

changes in the chronological figures in Genesis 5 and 11.[9] It was impossible to hold the view that the Flood of Noah would have taken place in the time when great Pharaohs and Mesopotamian kings ruled in the ancient Near East.[10] While there are only 292 years between the birth of Abraham and the Flood in the MT chronology the LXX chronology allows for 1172 years between the two events.[11]

The Septuagint chronology is mainly followed in Demetrius's chronological system, which is preserved in Eusebius's *Praeparatio evangelica*. Here the church historian quotes the works of Alexander Polyhistor who transmitted several Jewish chronographers' details.[12] Demetrius allows 3624 years 'from Adam until Joseph's brothers came into Egypt'. This figure corresponds well to the Septuagint figures, which are not totally coherent but allow 3604 years or exactly 3624 years between these two events.[13] Another length of the period in Demetrius's chronology is 1360

9. B.Z. Wacholder, 'Biblical Chronology in the Hellenistic World Chronicles', *HTR* 61 (1968), pp. 451-81.

10. For this see Larsson, 'The Chronology of the Pentateuch', esp. p. 403: 'The translators – probably working in Alexandria – must have known the official Egyptian chronology recorded by Manetho in the first half of the third century. According to this, the first "historical" pharaohs had lived almost 3000 years earlier. Consequently there could not have been a flood over the whole world just 2000 years earlier. The simplest way to avoid discussions and objections was to lengthen the time by adding another 100 years to the patriarchs' ages when they begat [= begot] their first sons.' It is also worth noting that in the fragment of Pseudo-Eupolemus preserved in Eusebius's *Praeparatio evangelica* 9.18.2 (*OTP*, II, p. 882) it is noted that according to some unknown (Babylonian?) source some giants – among them Belos – escaped from the Flood. Belos settled in Babylon and built a tower. By predating the Flood the Septuagint translation became readable because there were better possibilities to discuss the 'historical' setting of the catastrophe.

11. Hughes (*Secrets of the Times*, pp. 238-41) discusses different possibilities of relating the chronology of the LXX to the postexilic events.

12. This transmission of the texts of Demetrius as well as other Jewish chronographers via Alexander Polyhistor to Eusebius's work actualizes several questions of reliability of these chronological details. However, scholars have often regarded this transmission as reliable. For this see P.W. van der Horst, 'The Interpretation of the Bible by the Minor Hellenistic Jewish Authors', in J. Mulder (ed.), *The Literature of the Jewish People in the Period of the Second Temple and the Talmud*. I. *Mikra : Text, Translation, Reading and Interpretation of the Hebrew Bible in Ancient Judaism and Early Christianity* (Philadelphia: Fortress, 1988), pp. 519-46, esp. 519-20. See the English translations of the passages transmitted in Eusebius's *Praeparatio evangelica* in *OTP*, II, pp. 843-903.

13. In Codex Alexandrinus the chronology from Adam to the Flood is 20 years longer because according to it Methuselah was 187 (and not 167) years old when his son Lamech was born. It is this Alexandrian chronology which is followed in Demetrius's work. For this see Hughes, *Secrets of the Times*, pp. 238-42.

8. The Priestly Chronological Framework

years 'from the deluge until Jacob's coming into Egypt' which corresponds exactly to the chronological details in the Septuagint.

Another Jewish author whose chronological system is closer to that of the Septuagint rather than that of the Masoretic text is Eupolemus. In the fragment transmitted in the work of Clement of Alexandria (*Strom.* 1.141.4) Eupolemus writes that 'all the years from Adam to the fifth year of the reign of Demetrius (while Ptolemy was in his twelfth year as king of Egypt) are five thousand, one hundred and forty-nine, and from the time when Moses led the Jews out of Egypt to the aforementioned date there are two thousand, five hundred and eighty years'. Van der Horst notes that 'these numbers neither agree with MT nor with LXX'.[14] Bartlett writes that Eupolemus's way of dating the exodus and the time of Moses as 2580 years before his time was an attempt to show 'the Jews, with their wisdom and culture, were a much more ancient people than the Greeks'.[15] However, we must be careful to detect all available errors in the transmission process of these figures. It seems to me that we have a good reason to argue that an error has occurred in the transmission of the figures. Eupolemus calculates 5149 years from Adam to the fifth regnal year of Demetrius I Soter (= Ptolemy Euergetes II 12) i.e. 158/57 BCE, and 2580 years from the exodus to Demetrius 5. These figures imply that there would have been 2569 years from Adam to the exodus. However, the Septuagint chronological system calculates 3569 years from Adam to the entry of Jacob into Egypt, a period which is exactly 1000 years longer than Eupolemus's period from Adam to the exodus. In that case we may ask whether there are two mistakes in the chronological tradition transmitted by Clement of Alexandria. The first mistake is that the periods are calculated from Adam to Jacob's entry into Egypt and from that entry to Demetrius 5 respectively. The second mistake concerns the figure 2580 which should be 1580. In that case we should receive the following chronological details:

From Adam to Jacob's entry 3569 years (as in the Septuagint)
From Jacob's entry to Demetrius 5 1580 years

Can we explain the reasoning behind Eupolemus's way of calculating these 1580 years? I think we can. The Septuagint chronology allows for 215 years for Israel's time in Egypt (Exod. 12.40)[16], 440 years from

---

14. Van der Horst, 'Interpretation of the Bible', p. 539.
15. J.R. Bartlett, *Jews in the Hellenistic World: Josephus, Aristeas, the Sibylline Oracles, Eupolemus* (Cambridge: Cambridge University Press, 1985), p. 58.
16. The Septuagint version reads in Exod. 12.40 that Israelites will be in Egypt and in Canaan for 430 years. This information was then understood so that there

the exodus to the Temple building project of Solomon (1 Kgs 6.1), and 430 years from the temple building to its destruction i.e. 1085 years. What then remains is a period of 495 years which can be explained in such a way that the 490-year period of Dan. 9.24-27 was interpreted as the period from the exile to the Maccabean time about 164/63 BCE when the Temple was purified. The remaining short period between 164/63 BCE and 158/57 BCE is about 5 years. Eupolemus may have been the same person as Eupolemus, the son of John, mentioned in 1 Macc. 8.17-18 (cf. 2 Macc. 4.11). If this is the case, we may assume that Eupolemus was well aware of the calculations in Dan. 9.24-27 and indeed regarded 490 years to be the corresponding period from the exile to the dedication of the Temple. If this, in turn, is the case, we have good reason to argue that even Eupolemus followed the Septuagint chronological system.

The Septuagint chronological system was apparently created to fix the biblical periods in Genesis 1–11 to earlier dates. On the other hand, it was also possible to argue for the main apologetic argument that Moses was the first wise man and the grounder of civilization[17] by means of the Masoretic chronology. In both systems the exodus took place about 900 years before the destruction of the Temple, and clearly before the Greek civilization.

The Masoretic chronological system was followed by Jewish groups which did not meet the challenge of world chroniclers. A good example is the Book of Jubilees which mainly built up its chronological system on the data in the Masoretic text.[18]

---

were two 215 year periods, the first one was in Egypt and the second one in Canaan. For this reasoning see Hughes, *Secrets of the Times*, pp. 32-36.

17. This argument is most clearly visible in Artapanus's and Eupolemus's texts. See Bartlett, *Jews in the Hellenistic World*, pp. 56-71, esp. 59-61; van der Horst, 'Minor Hellenistic Jewish Authors', p. 537.

18. For the chronological system in Jubilees and its details see in particular J. VanderKam, 'Das chronologische Konzept des Jubiläenbuches', *ZAW* 107 (1995), pp. 80–100 which is also published as an English version 'Studies in the Chronology of the Book of Jubilees', in J. VanderKam, *From Revelation to Canon: Studies in the Hebrew Bible and Second Temple Literature* (JSJSup, 62; Leiden: Brill, 2000), pp. 522-44. An important complement to VanderKam's explanations is M. Segal, 'The Literary Relationship between the Genesis Apocryphon and Jubilees: The Chronology of Abram and Sarai's Descent to Egypt', *Aramaic Studies* 8 (2010), pp. 71-88. Segal gives a good explanation on conflicting chronological data of Jubilees concerning the history of Abraham.

Hughes has tried to explain the outcome of the chronological system of the Masoretic text. He argues that because the birth of Arpachsdad is insecure, the chronology in the Masoretic text may also be 1946 AM for the birth of Abraham. In that case we receive the following dates for the biblical events:

The Flood	1656 AM
Abraham	1946/48 AM
The Entry into Egypt	2236/38 AM
The Exodus	2666/68 AM
The Foundation of the Temple	3146/48 AM
The Destruction of the Temple	3576/78 AM

Hughes calculates 424 years after the destruction of the Temple (587 BCE) at which point we are in the time of the rededication of the Temple in the Maccabean time (164 BCE) which corresponds to the date 3999 AM, i.e. about 4000 years from Creation. Hughes admits that such a theory has its difficulties because we do not know how ancient Jewish chronographers calculated the intertestamental period – something which is well marshaled by the chronological system of Josephus (based in Dan. 9.24-27) as well as in Demetrius's chronology.[19] To date the Masoretic chronological tradition to the Maccabean period is problematic. We have seen in the previous chapter that the chronological details now available in the Masoretic text do not support the dating of the foundation of the First Temple to 480 years after the exodus. This being the case Hughes's theory also presupposes a certain kind of calculation of the Masoretic numbers. Because of this internal tension in the 480-year calculation in the Deuteronomistic History and the insecure information regarding the length of the postexilic period, the best explanation is that the Masoretic chronological system was established before the Maccabean period.

---

19. Hughes, *Secrets of the Times*, pp. 233-37. It is worth noting that Hughes writes 323 years on p. 234, but he apparently means 423 years!

9

CONCLUSIONS

The aim of this study was to deal with the biblical chronology and early Jewish chronological systems and explain the reasoning which led to their outcome. We have shown that the chronological records of the kings of Judah and Israel during the period between 930 BCE and 586 BCE are based on reliable annalistic records which must originate from royal archives. However, the authors of the present form of the Books of Kings did not receive their chronological traditions direct from royal archives. We have argued that after the destruction of Samaria, synchronic chronological presentations of the history of Judah and Israel were composed and the Deuteronomistic editors used them. They made their own conclusions from the source material and created their own chronology which sometimes became contradictory – a fact which is detectable in the present form of the Hebrew Bible. In particular, we have shown that these chronological problems concern the end of the dynasty of Omri and the beginning of the dynasty of Jehu, the beginning of the reign of Uzziah and finally also the length of the reign of Pekah.

We have presented arguments for that the chronological traditions of Israelite and Judean kings can be put in harmony with the Assyrian and Babylonian records and thus connect to our absolute chronology – something which indicates that we have a reliable tradition in the Hebrew Bible. The only problematic issue is the reign of Hezekiah and the question whether it postdates the fall of Samaria or overlaps with it:

Israel		Judah	
Jeroboam I	930/29–909/08	Rehoboam	930/29–914/13
Nadab	909/08–908/07	Abiam	913/12–910/09
Baasha	908/07–885/84	Asa	910/09–870/69
Elah	885/84–884/83	Jehoshaphat	870/69–847/46
Zimri	884/83	Jehoram	847/46–846/45
Omri	884/83–873/72	Ahaziah	846/45
Ahab	873/72–852/51	Athaliah	845/44–840/39

9. Conclusions

Ahaziah	852/51–851/50	Joash	840/39–801/00
Jehoram	851/50–845/44	Amaziah	801/00–787/86
Jehu	845/44–818/17	Uzziah	786/85–735/34
Jehoahaz	818/17–802/01	Jotham	750/49–735/34 (2 Kgs 15:5)
Jehoash	802/01–787/86	Ahaz	735/34–716/15
Jeroboam II	787/86–747/46	Hezekiah	715/14–697/96
Zechariah	747/46	Manasseh	697/96–643/42
Shallum	746/45	Amon	643/42–641/40
Menahem	746/45–737/36	Josiah	641/40–610/09
Pekahiah	737/36–735/34	Jehoahaz	609
Pekah	735/34–732/31	Jehoiakim	609/08–598/97
Hosea	731/30–723/22	Jeconiah	598 (Dec)–597 (March)
		Zedekiah	597–586

We have also demonstrated how the later Jewish chronological traditions attested in Josephus are based on Dan. 9.24-27. Therefore, it is out of question to use the chronological traditions of Josephus to any historical construction as far as the length of the postexilic periods are concerned.

We have demonstrated that the chronology of Demetrius seems to contain a 26/27 year difference to our absolute chronology, and by using this record we may explain the chronological system of the Damascus Document at Qumran and in Second Baruch. It is reasonable to assume that this difference is partly connected with the fact that the actual length of the exile was only 49 years while the prophecy of Jeremiah indicated that it would last for 70 years.

We provided an explanation for the outcome of the seventy yearweeks in Dan. 9.24-27. We argued that 7 yearweeks (49 years) refers to the length of the exile (586–538/7 BCE) and 62 yearweeks (434 years) parallel to the length of the reigns of Judean kings from Solomon to Zedekiah i.e. the chronological data in the books of Kings. The remaining 7 years refer to the length of the last decisive eschatological struggle. This explanation indicates that the 70 yearweeks in Dan. 9.24-27 are an artificial construction before the Maccabean time and was used then to justify the Maccabean wars as the decisive eschatological battle. Later this artificial construction was used by Eupolemus and Josephus for their chronologies.

Finally, we have dealt with the chronological systems of the pre-monarchic Israel. We argued that the 480 year period in 1 Kgs 6.1 and the 300 year period in Judg. 11.26 may belong to the same pre-Deuteronomistic chronological tradition. Neither figure is in harmony with the present chronology of the Deuteronomistic History. We have presented a view as to how these figures can be put in harmony with other chronological details which the Deuteronomistic writers adopted from earlier traditions. Nevertheless, the chronology of pre-monarchic Israel is at best an artificial construction not based in any archival sources and therefore cannot be a solid basis for research of the history of Israel.

When the translation process of the Hebrew Bible into Greek began during the third century BCE the chronological details in Genesis 5 and 11 were fixed so that they could better correspond to the historical periods of world chronicles such as Manetho (for Egypt) and Berossus (for Mesopotamia). This procedure explains the great difference between the Masoretic and Septuagint texts in Genesis 5 and 11.

BIBLIOGRAPHY

Albright, W.F., 'The Chronology of the Divided Monarchy of Israel', *BASOR* 100 (1945), pp. 16-22.
—'Further Light on Synchronisms between Egypt and Asia in the Period 935–685 BC', *BASOR* 130 (1956), pp. 23-27.
—'New Light from Egypt on the Chronology and History of Israel and Judah', *BASOR* 130 (1953), pp. 4-11.
—'The Seal of Eliakim and the Latest Preexilic History of Judah with Some Observations on Ezekiel', *JBL* 51 (1932), pp. 77-106.
Amit, Y., *The Book of Judges: The Art of Editing* (Leiden: Brill, 1999).
—*History and ideology: An Introduction to Historiography in the Hebrew Bible* (Sheffield: Sheffield Academic Press, 1999).
—*Judges: Introduction and Commentary* (Mikar LeYisra'el; Tel Aviv: Am Oved, 1999 [Hebrew]).
Andersen, K.T., 'Die Chronologie der Könige von Israel und Juda', *ST* 23 (1969), pp. 69-114.
—'Noch einmal: Die Chronologie der Königen von Israel und Juda', *SJOT* 3 (1989), pp. 1-45.
Athas, G., 'Setting the Record Straight: What Are We Making of the Tel Dan Inscription?', *JSS* 51 (2006), pp. 241-55.
—*The Tel Dan Inscription: A Reappraisal and a New Interpretation* (London: T. & T. Clark, 2003).
Avigad, N., and B. Sass, *Corpus of West Semitic Stamp Seals* (Jerusalem: The Israel Academy of Sciences and Humanities, 1997).
Bartlett, J.R., *Jews in the Hellenistic World: Josephus, Aristeas, the Sibylline Oracles, Eupolemus* (Cambridge: Cambridge University Press, 1985).
Begrich, J., *Die Chronologie der Könige von Israel und Juda und die Quellen des Rahmens der Königsbücher* (Tübingen: Mohr Siebeck, 1929).
—'Jes 14, 28-32: Ein Beitrag zur Chronologie der israelitisch-judäischen Königszeit', in W. Zimmerli (ed.), *Joachim Begrich: Gesammelte Studien zum Alten Testament* (TB, 21; Munich: Kaiser, 1964), pp. 121-31.
Bergsma, J.S., 'The Restored Temple as "Built Jubilee" in Ezekiel 40–48', *Proceedings of the Eastern Great Lakes and Midwest Biblical Society* 24 (2004), pp. 75-85.
Bickerman, E.J., *Chronology of the Ancient World* (London: Thames & Hudson, rev. edn, 1980).
Biran, A., and J. Naveh, 'An Aramaic Stele Fragment from Tel Dan', *IEJ* 43 (1993), pp. 81-93.
—'The Tel Dan Inscription: A New Fragment', *IEJ* 45 (1995), pp. 1-18.

Blum, E., 'Solomon and the United Monarchy: Some Textual Evidence', in R. Kratz and H. Spieckermann (eds.), *One God – One Cult – One Nation: Archaeological and Biblical Perspectives* (BZAW, 405; Berlin: W. de Gruyter, 2010), pp. 69-78.
Bright, J., *A History of Israel* (Louisville: Westminster/John Knox Press, 2000).
Budde, K., 'Zum Eingang des Buches Ezechiel', *JBL* 50 (1931), pp. 20-41.
Callaway, P.R., *The History of the Qumran Community: An Investigation* (JSPSup, 3; Sheffield: Sheffield Academic Press, 1988).
Carr, D.M., *Writings on the Tablet of the Heart: Origins of Scripture and Literature* (New York: Oxford University Press, 2011).
Cazelles, H., '587 ou 586?', in C.L. Meyers and M. O'Connor (eds.), *The Word of the Lord Shall Go Forth* (Winona Lake: Eisenbrauns, 1983), pp. 427-35.
Clines, D.J.A., 'The Evidence for an Autumnal New Year in Pre-exilic Israel Reconsidered', *JBL* 93 (1974), pp. 22-40.
—*Ezra, Nehemiah, Esther* (NCB; Grand Rapids: Eerdmans, 1984).
Collins, J.J., *Daniel: A Commentary on the Book of Daniel* (Hermeneia; Minneapolis: Fortress Press, 1993).
Cogan, M., and H. Tadmor, *II Kings* (AB, 11; New York: Doubleday & Co., 1988).
Cross, F.M., *The Ancient Library of Qumran and Modern Biblical Studies* (Sheffield: Sheffield Academic Press, 1995).
Davies, P., *The Damascus Covenant: An Interpretation of the 'Damascus Covenant'* (JSOTSup, 25; Sheffield: Sheffield Academic Press, 1983).
Demsky, A., 'Literacy', in E.M. Meyers, *The Oxford Encyclopedia of Archaeology in the Near East*, III (Oxford: Oxford University Press, 1997), pp. 362-69.
—*Literacy in Ancient Israel* (The Biblical Encyclopaedia Library, 28; Jerusalem: Bialik Institute, 2012 [Hebrew]).
—'Writing in Ancient Israel Part One: The Biblical Period', in M.J. Mulder (ed.), *Mikra: Text, Translation, Reading and Interpretation of the Hebrew Bible in Ancient Judaism and early Christianity* (Assen/Maastricht: Van Gorcum, 1988), pp. 2-20.
Dietrich, W., *Die frühe Königszeit in Israel: 10. Jahrhundert v.Chr* (Bibliche Enzyklopädie, 3: Stuttgart: Kohlhammer, 1997).
Finegan, J., *Handbook of Biblical Chronology: Principles of Time Reckoning in the Ancient World and Problems of Chronology in the Bible* (Peabody: Hendrickson, rev. edn, 1998).
Finkelstein, I., and N.A. Silberman, *David and Solomon: In Search of the Bible's Sacred Kings and the Roots of the Western Tradition* (New York: Free Press, 2006).
Galil, G., *The Chronology of the Kings of Israel and Judah* (Studies in the History and Culture of the Ancient Near East, 9; Leiden: Brill, 1996).
—'Dates and Calendars', in Lemaire and Halpern (eds.), *The Books of Kings*, pp. 427-43.
—'Review of M.C. Tetley, The Reconstructed Chronology of the Divided Kingdom', *CBQ* 68 (2006), pp. 131-33.
Gooding, D.W, 'Review', *JTS* 21 (1970), pp. 118-31.
Gray, J., *1 and 2 Kings: A Commentary* (OTL; London: SCM Press, 1970).
Grayson, A.K., *Assyrian and Babylonian Chronicles* (Texts from Cuneiform Sources; Locust Valley: J.J. Augustin, 1975).
—*Assyrian Rulers of the Early First Millennium BC II (858–745 BC)* (RIMA, 3; Toronto: University of Toronto Press, 1996).

Green, A.R., 'The Chronology of the Last Days of Judah: Two Apparent Discrepancies', *JBL* 101 (1982), pp. 57-73.
Halpern, B., *David's Secret Demons: Messiah, Murderer, Traitor, King* (The Bible in its World; Atlanta: Scholars Press, 2001).
Halpern, B., and A. Lemaire, 'The Composition of Kings', in Lemaire and Halpern (eds.), *The Books of Kings*, pp. 123-53.
Hanson, P., *Dawn of Apocalyptic* (Philadelphia: Fortress Press, 1975).
Hartman, L.F., and A. DiLella, *The Book of Daniel* (AB, 23; New York: Doubleday, 1978).
Hayes, J.H., and P.K. Hooker, *A New Chronology for the Kings of Israel and Judah and its Implications for the Biblical History and Literature* (Atlanta: John Knox Press, 1988).
Herrmann, J., *Ezechiel* (KAT, 11; Leipzig/Erlangen: Deichert, 1924).
Hoffmeier, J.K., *Ancient Israel in Sinai: The Evidence for the Authenticity of the Wilderness Tradition* (Oxford: Oxford University Press, 2005).
—*Israel in Egypt: The Evidence for the Authenticity of the Exodus Tradition* (Oxford: Oxford University Press, 1996).
Hughes, J., *Secrets of the Times: Myth and History in Biblical Chronology* (JSOTSup, 66; Sheffield: Sheffield Academic Press, 1990).
Jacobus, H.R., 'The Curse of Cainan (Jub. 8.1-5): Genealogies in Genesis 5 and Genesis 11 and a Mathematical Pattern', *JSP* 18 (2009), pp. 207-32.
Jamieson-Drake, D.W., *Scribes and Schools in Monarchic Judah: A Socio-Archaeological Approach* (The Social World of Biblical Antiquity Series, 9; JSOTSup, 109; Sheffield: Sheffield Academic Press, 1991).
Jepsen, A., *Die Quellen des Königsbuches* (Halle: Niemeyer, 1953).
—'Ein Neuer Fixpunkt für die Chronologie der israelitischen Könige?', *VT* 20 (1970), pp. 359-61.
—'Zur Chronologie der Könige von Israel und Juda', in A. Jepsen and R. Hanhart, *Untersuchungen zur israelitisch-jüdischen Chronologie* (BZAW, 88; Berlin: W. de Gruyter, 1964), pp. 4-48.
Kitchen, K.A., 'Egypt, History of (Chronology)', in *ABD*, II, pp. 322-31.
—*The Third Intermediate Period in Egypt (1100–650 B.C.)* (Warminster: Aris & Phillips, 1973).
Klein, R.W., 'Archaic Chronologies and the Textual History of the Old Testament', *HTR* 67 (1974), pp. 255-63.
Koch, K., *Das Buch Daniel* (EdF, 144; Darmstadt: Wissenschaftliche Buchgesellschaft, 1980).
—*Daniel* (BKAT, 22/1; Neukirchen-Vluyn: Neukirchener Verlag, 1986).
—'Die mysteriösen Zahlen der judäischen Könige und die apokalyptischen Jahrwochen', *VT* 28 (1978), pp. 433-41.
Kratz, R., 'The Visions of Daniel', in J.J. Collins and P.W. Flint (eds.), *The Book of Daniel: Composition and Reception*, I (VTSup, 83; Leiden: Brill, 2001), pp. 91-113.
Kuhrt, A., *The Ancient Near East c. 3000–330 BC*, I–II (London/New York: Routledge, 1995).

Kutsch, E., *Die Chronologischen Daten des Ezechielbuches* (OBO, 62; Freiburg: Universitätsverlag, 1985).
—'Das Jahr der katastrophe: 587 v. Chr. Kritische Erwägungen zu neueren chronologischen Veruschen', *Biblica* 55 (1974), pp. 520-45 (repr. in E. Kutsch, *Kleine Schriften zum Alten Testament zum 65. Geburtstag* [ed. L. Schmidt and K. Eberlein; BZAW, 168; Berlin: W. de Gruyter, 1986), pp. 3-28.
Laato, A., '*About Zion I will not be silent'*: *The Book of Isaiah as an Ideological Unity* (ConBOT, 44; Stockholm: Almqvist & Wiksell International, 1998).
—'The Chronology of the Damascus Document of Qumran', *RdQ* 60 (1992), pp. 605-607.
—*Josiah and David Redivivus: The Historical Josiah and the Messianic Expectations of Exilic and Postexilic Times* (ConBOT, 33; Stockholm: Almqvist & Wiksell International, 1992).
—'The Levitical Genealogies in 1 Chr 6 and the Formation of the Levitical Ideology in Postexilic Judah', *JSOT* 62 (1994), pp. 77-99.
—*A Star Is Rising: The Historical Development of the Old Testament Royal Ideology and the Rise of the Jewish Messianic Expectations* (International Studies in Formative Christianity and Judaism; Atlanta: Scholars Press, 1997).
Lacocque, A., *The Book of Daniel* (London: SPCK, 1979).
Lang, B., *Ezechiel: Der Prophet und das Buch* (EdF, 153; Darmstadt: Wissenschaftliche Buchgesellschaft, 1981).
Larsson, G., 'The Chronology of the Kings of Israel and Judah as a System', *ZAW* 114 (2002), pp. 224-35.
—'The Chronology of the Pentateuch: A Comparison of the MT and LXX', *JBL* 102 (1983), pp. 401-409.
—'Septuagint versus Massoretic Chronology', *ZAW* 114 (2002), pp. 511-21.
Lemaire, A., and B. Halpern (eds.), *The Books of Kings: Sources, Composition, Historiography and Reception* (VTSup, 129; Leiden: Brill, 2010).
Lemche, N.P., *Ancient Israel: A New History of Israelite Society* (Sheffield: Sheffield Academic Press, 1988).
Levey, S.H., *The Targum of Ezekiel* (The Aramaic Bible, 13; Wilmington: Michael Glazier, 1987).
Lewy, J., *Die Chronologie der Könige von Israel und Juda* (Giessen: Alfred Töpelmann, 1927).
Lim, T., 'Wicked Priest', in L.H. Schiffman and J.C. VanderKam (eds.), *Encyclopedia of the Dead Sea Scrolls* (2 vols.; Oxford: Oxford University Press, 2000), II, pp. 973-76.
Malamat, A., *History of Biblical Israel: Major Problems and Minor Issues* (Leiden: Brill, 2004).
—'The Last Kings of Judah and the Fall of Jerusalem', *IEJ* 18 (1968), pp. 137-56.
—'The Twilight of Judah in the Egyptian-Babylonian Maelstrom', in J.A. Emerton (ed.), *Congress Volume: Edinburgh 1974* (VTSup, 28; Leiden: Brill, 1975), pp. 123-45 (reproduced in A. Malamat, *The History of Biblical Israel* [Leiden: Brill, 2004], pp. 299-321).
Marti, K., *Das Buch Daniel* (KH-CAT, 18; Tübingen: Mohr, 1901).
—*Das Dodekapropheton* (KH-CAT, 13/2; Tübingen: Mohr, 1904).
Mazar, E., D. Ben-Shlomo, and S. Ahituv, 'An Inscribed Pithos From the *Ophel*', *IEJ* 63 (2013), pp. 39-49.

McCarter, P.K., 'The Apology of David', *JBL* 99 (1980), pp. 489-504.
—' "Plots, True of False": The Succession Narrative as Court Apologetic', *Interpretation* 35 (1981), pp. 355-67.
McComiskey, T.E., 'The Seventy "Weeks" of Daniel Against the Background of Ancient Near Eastern Literature', *WTJ* 47 (1985), pp. 18-45.
McFall, L., 'Review of M.C. Tetley, The Reconstructed Chronology of the Divided Kingdom', *VT* 57 (2007), pp. 574-75.
Millard, A., *The Eponyms of the Assyrian Empire 910–612 BC* (SAAS, 2; Helsinki: The Neo-Assyrian Text Corpus Project, 1994).
—'The Ostracon from the Days of David Found at Khirbet Qeiyafa', *Tyndale Bulletin* 62 (2011), pp. 1–14.
—'Owners and Users of Hebrew Seals', *EI* 26 (1999), pp. 129-33.
Miller, J.M., and J.H. Hayes, *A History of Ancient Israel and Judah* (Philadelphia: The Westminster Press, 1986).
Mitchell, H.G., *A Critical and Exegetical Commentary on Haggai and Zechariah* (ICC; Edinburgh: T. & T. Clark, 1912).
Montgomery, J.A., *A Critical and Exegetical Commentary on the Book of Daniel* (ICC; Edinburgh: T. & T. Clark, 1927).
Murnane, W.J., *Ancient Egyptian Coregencies* (SAOC, 40; Chicago: The Oriental Institute, 1977).
Na'aman, N., 'The "Conquest of Canaan" in the Book of Joshua and in History', in I. Finkelstein and N. Na'aman (eds.), *From Nomadism to Monarchy: Archaeological and Historical Aspects of Early Israel* (Jerusalem: Yad Izhak Ben-Zvi, 1994), pp. 218-81.
—'Historical and Chronological Notes on the Kingdoms of Israel and Judah in the Eight Century B.C.', *VT* 36 (1986), pp. 71-92.
—'Israel, Edom and Egypt in the 10th Century B.C.E.', *TA* 19 (1992), pp. 71-93.
—'Sennacherib's "Letter to God" on his Campaign to Judah', *BASOR* 214 (1974), pp. 25-39.
—'Shishak's Campaign to Palestine as Reflected by the Epigraphic, Biblical and Archaeological Evidence', *Zion* 63 (1998), pp. 247-76 (Hebrew).
—'Solomon's District List (1 Kings 4:7-19) and the Assyrian Province System in Palestine', *UF* 33 (2001), pp. 419-36.
Neusner, J., *Messiah in Context: Israel's History and Destiny in Formative Judaism* (Philadelphia: Fortress Press, 1984).
Niemann, H.M., *Herrschaft, Königtum und Staat: Skizzen zur soziokulturellen Entwicklung im monarchischen Israel* (FAT, 6; Tübingen: Mohr Siebeck, 1993).
Nowack, W., *Die kleinen Propheten* (HAT, 3/4, 369; Göttingen: Vandenhoeck & Ruprecht, 1922).
Parker, R.A., *The Calendars of Ancient Egypt* (Studies in Ancient Oriental Civilization, 26; Chicago: University of Chicago Press, 1950).
Parker, R.A., and W.H. Dubberstein, *Babylonian Chronology 626 B.C.–A.D. 75* (Brown University Studies, 19; Providence: Brown University Press, 1956).
Pavlovsky, V., and E. Vogt, 'Die Jahre der Könige von Juda und Israel', *Biblica* 45 (1964), pp. 321-47.
Plöger, O., *Das Buch Daniel* (KAT, 18; Gütersloh: Mohn, 1962).
Porteous, N.W., *Das Danielbuch* (ATD, 23; Göttingen: Vandenhoeck & Ruprecht, 1962).

Puech, E., 'L'ostracon de Khirbet Qeyafa et les débuts de la royauté en Israël', *Revue Biblique* 117 (2010), pp. 162-84.
Rabinowitz, I., 'A Reconsideration of "Damascus" and "390 Years" in the "Damascus" ("Zadokite") Fragments', *JBL* 73 (1954), pp. 11-35.
Reade, J., *Mesopotamian Guidelines for Biblical Chronology* (Monographi Journals of the Near East, Syro-Mesopotamian Studies 4/1 May, 1981).
Redditt, P.L., 'Daniel 9: Its Structure and Meaning', *CBQ* 62 (2000), pp. 236-49.
Reicke, B., *Neutestamentliche Zeitgeschichte. Die biblische Welt von 500 v.Chr. bis 100 n.Chr* (Berlin: W. de Gruyter, 3rd rev. edn, 1982).
Rendsburg, G., 'On the Writing of *bytdwd* in the Aramaic Inscription of Tel Dan', *IEJ* 45 (1995), pp. 22-25.
Roddy, N., ' "Two Parts: Weeks of Seven Weeks": The End of the Age as *Terminus ad Quem* for *2 Baruch*', *JSP* 14 (1996), pp. 3-14.
Rollston, C.A., 'The Khirbet Qeiyafa Ostracon: Methodological Musings and Caveats', *TA* 38 (2011), pp. 67-82.
—*Writing and Literacy in the World of Ancient Israel: Epigraphic Evidence from the Iron Age* (Atlanta: Society of Biblical Literature, 2010).
Rowley, H.H., *The Zadokite Fragments and the Dead Sea Scrolls* (Oxford: Blackwell, 1952).
Rudolph, W., *Haggai – Sacharja 1-8 – Sacharja 9-14 – Maleachi* (KAT, 13/4; Gütersloh: Gutersloher Verlagshaus Mohn, 1976).
Sanders, S.L., *The Invention of Hebrew* (Urbana and Chicago: University of Illinois Press, 2009).
Schniedewind, W.M., *How the Bible Became a Book: The Textualization of Ancient Israel* (Cambridge: Cambridge University Press, 2004).
—'Tel Dan Stela: New Light on Aramaic and Jehu's Revolt', *BASOR* 302 (1996), pp. 75-90.
Schürer, E., *Geschichte des jüdischen Volkes im Zeitalter Jesu Christi*, III (Leipzig, 4th edn, 1909).
Segal, M., 'The Literary Relationship between the Genesis Apocryphon and Jubilees: The Chronology of Abram and Sarai's Descent to Egypt', *Aramaic Studies* 8 (2010), pp. 71-88.
Shea, W.H., 'The Date and Significance of the Samaria Ostraca', *IEJ* 27 (1977), pp. 16-27.
Shedl, C., 'Nochmals das Jahr der Zerströrung Jerusalems: 587 oder 586 v. Chr.', *ZAW* 74 (1962), pp. 209-213.
—'Textkritische Bemerkungen zu den Synchronismen der Könige von Israel und Juda', *VT* 12 (1962), pp. 88-119.
Shenkel, J.D., *Chronology and Recensional Development in the Greek Text of Kings* (Cambridge, MA: Harvard University Press, 1968).
Stade, B., 'Deuterozacharja. Eine kritische Studie', *ZAW* 1 (1881), pp. 1-96.
Steck, O.H., Überlieferung und Zeitgeschichte in den Elia-Erzählungen (WMANT, 26; Neukirchen–Vluyn: Neukirchener Verlag, 1968).
Stenring, K., *The Enclosed Garden* (Stockholm: Almqvist & Wiksell, 1966).
Strand, K.A., 'Thiele's Biblical Chronology as a Corrective for Extrabiblical Dates', *Andrews University Seminary Studies* 34 (1996), pp. 295-317.
Strange, J., 'Joram, King of Israel and Judah', *VT* 25 (1975), pp. 191-201.

Tadmor, H., 'The Chronology of the First Temple Period: A Presentation and Evaluation of the Sources', in A. Malamat (ed.), *The Age of the Monarchies: Political History* (The World History of the Jewish People, 4/1; Jerusalem: Massada, 1979), pp. 44-60.
—*The Inscriptions of Tiglath-Pileser III King of Assyria* (Jerusalem: The Israel Academy of Sciences and Humanities, 1994).
Talmon, S., *King, Cult and Calendar in Ancient Israel: Collected Studies* (Jerusalem: Magnes Press, The Hebrew University, 1986).
Tappy, R.E., and P.K. McCarter, *Literate Culture and Tenth-Century Canaan: The Tel Zayit Abecedary in Context* (Winona Lake: Eisenbrauns, 2008).
Tappy, R.E., P.K. McCarter, M.J. Lundberg, and B. Zuckerman, 'An Abecedary of the Mid-Tenth Century B.C.E. from the Judean Shephelah', *BASOR* 344 (2006), pp. 5-46.
Taylor, S.G., 'A Reconsideration of the "Thirtieth Year" in Ezekiel 1:1', *Tyndale Bulletin* 17 (1966), pp. 119-20.
Tetley, M.C., *Reconstructed Chronology of the Divided Kingdom* (Winona Lake: Eisenbrauns, 2005).
Thiele, E.R., *A Chronology of the Hebrew Kings* (Grand Rapids: Zondervan, 1982).
—'The Chronology of the Kings of Judah and Israel', *JNES* 3 (1944), pp. 137-86.
—'Coregencies and Overlapping Reigns among the Hebrew Kings', *JBL* 93 (1974), pp. 174-200.
—*The Mysterious Numbers of the Hebrew Kings. A Reconstruction of the Chronology of the Kingdoms of Israel and Judah* (Chicago: University of Chicago Press, 1951).
Torrey, C.C., *Pseudo-Ezekiel and the Original Prophecy* (Yale Oriental Series Researches, 18; New Haven: Yale University Press, 1930; repr. New York, 1970).
van der Horst, P.W., 'The Interpretation of the Bible by the Minor Hellenistic Jewish Authors', in J. Mulder (ed.), *The Literature of the Jewish People in the Period of the Second Temple and the Talmud. I. Mikra: Text, Translation, Reading and Interpretation of the Hebrew Bible in Ancient Judaism and Early Christianity* (Philadelphia: Fortress Press, 1988), pp. 519-46.
vanderKam, J., 'Das chronologische Konzept des Jubiläenbuches', *ZAW* 107 (1995), pp. 80-100.
—'Studies in the Chronology of the Book of Jubilees', in VanderKam, *From Revelation to Canon: Studies in the Hebrew Bible and Second Temple Literature* (JSJSup, 62; Leiden: Brill, 2000), pp. 522-44.
van der Toorn, K., *Scribal Culture and the Making of the Hebrew Bible* (Cambridge, MA: Harvard University Press, 2007).
De Vaux, R., *Ancient Israel: Its Life and Institutions* (Grand Rapids: Eerdmans, 1997).
Vermes, G., *The Dead Sea Scrolls: Qumran in Perspective* (London: SCM Press, 1994).
Vogt, E., 'Die Neubabylonische Chronik über die Schlacht bei Karkemisch und die Einnahme von Jerusalem', in *Volume du Congrès Strassbourg 1956* (VTSup, 4; Leiden: Brill, 1956), pp. 67-96.
Wacholder, B.Z., 'Biblical Chronology in the Hellenistic World Chronicles', *HTR* 61 (1968), pp. 451-81.
—'Pseudo-Eupolemus' Two Greek Fragments on the Life of Abraham', *HUCA* 34 (1963), pp. 83-113.
Waddell, W.G., *Manetho* (LCL, 350; Cambridge, MA: Harvard University Press, 1980).

Weippert, H., 'Die "deuteronomistischen" Beurteilungen der Könige von Israel und Juda und das Problem der Redaktion der Königsbücher', *Biblica* 53 (1972), pp. 301-39.

—'Das deuteronomistische Geshichtswerk: sein Ziel und Ende in der neueren Forschung', *Theologische Rundschau* NF 50 (1985), pp. 213-49.

Wellhausen, J., *Die kleine Propheten übersetzt und erklärt* (Berlin: W. de Gruyter, 1963).

—*Prolegomena zur Geschichte Israels* (Berlin: W. de Gruyter, 1927).

Westermann, C., *A Continental Commentary: Genesis 1–11* (Minneapolis: Fortress Press, 1994).

Whitley, C.F., 'The "Thirtieth" Year in Ezekiel I 1', *VT* 9 (1959), pp. 326-30.

Wiesenberg, E., 'Chronological Data in the Zadokite Fragments', *VT* 5 (1955), pp. 284-308.

Williamson, H.G.M., *1 and Chronicles* (Grand Rapids: Eerdmans, 1982).

Wiseman, D.J., *Chronicles of Chaldean Kings (626–556 B.C.) in the British Museum* (London: The Trustees of the British Museum, 1956).

Yadin, Y., *Bar-Kokhba: The Rediscovery of the Legendary Hero of the Last Jewish Revolt Against Imperial Rome* (London: Weidenfeld & Nicolson, 1971).

Zimmerli, W., *Ezekiel 1* (Hermeneia; Philadelphia: Fortress Press, 1979).

Indexes

Index of References

HEBREW BIBLE/
OLD TESTAMENT
Genesis
1–11	110
5	114
5.1-28	106-11
5.30-32	106
7.6	106
9.28-29	106
11	114
11.10-26	106-11
11.32	106
15.13	98
15.16	98

Exodus
12.40	98, 109
23.10-11	14
23.14-17	14
34.18-23	14

Leviticus
23	15
25	14, 16, 59
25.8-10	59

Numbers
10.11	100
13.26-27	100

Deuteronomy
15	14

Joshua
14.6-15	100, 102
14.10-11	100

Judges
3.8	100
3.11	100
3.14	100
4.3	100
5.31	100
6.1	100
8.28	100
9.22	100
10.2	100
10.3	100
10.8	100
11.26	98, 101-104, 113
12.7	101
12.9	101
12.11	101
12.14	101
13.1	101
15.20	101

1 Samuel
4.18	101

2 Samuel
5.4-5	101
5.7-8	95

1 Kings
6.1	14, 16, 90, 98, 100-104, 110, 113
6.37-38	14, 16
8.2	16
11.41	25
14.2	6
14.19	25
14.20	18, 26
14.21	5, 26
14.25	8, 26, 64
14.29	25
15.1-2	17-18, 26
15.7	25
15.9-10	17-18, 26
15.23	25
15.25	17-18, 26
15.33	26-27
16.5	25, 27
16.6	27
16.8	26-27
16.14	25
16.20	25
16.22	27
16.23	27
16.27	25
16.28	27
16.29	27, 42
19.15-18	44
20	64-65
20.34	65
22	10-12, 40, 64-65
22.26	65
22.39	25
22.41-42	18, 27
22.46	25
22.52	18, 42

2 Kings
1.17-18	42
1.17	27, 29, 38, 40-41
1.18	25

2 Kings (cont.)		15.26	25	24.12	57-58, 69-70
3.1	27, 29, 38, 41-43	15.27	18, 28, 44-46	25	16, 30
3.13-14	44	15.29	30	25.1-9	69
8.7-15	65	15.30	28, 45-46, 48	25.8	55
8.16-17	27, 38, 40			25.9	57
8.16	42	15.31	25		
8.18	39	15.32-33	28, 45	*Isaiah*	
8.23	25	15.32	21, 44	7.1-17	30
8.25-26	28, 41-42	15.36	25	10.10-12	48
8.26	40	16.1-9	30	14.28-32	12, 47-48
9	66	16.1-2	29-30, 45-46	36–37	30
9.1-37	65			36.1	4
9.1-13	44	16.1	21, 44	36.19-20	48
9.14-28	39	16.8-9	67	38	62
9.29	28, 41-42	16.19	25	40–55	102
10.34	25	17–19	68		
11.4	28	17.1-6	13, 30	*Jeremiah*	
12.1-2	28	17.1	21-22, 29-30, 46-47	2.2	102
12.1	28, 37			2.6	102
12.20	25	17.4-6	31	22.24-30	60
13-15	36	17.6	4, 29	25.1-14	98
13.1	28	18.1-2	29-30, 46, 62	25.11-12	90
13.8	25			29.10	90
13.10	28	18.1	21	36.30-31	60
13.12	25	18.4	48	36.22-23	16
14.1	28	18.9-11	30-31, 46	36.22	14
14.15	25	18.9-10	4, 9, 12-13, 29	46.2	30, 52, 69
14.17	35			52.4-12	69-70
14.18	25	18.9	29	52.12	57
14.23	22, 28	18.10	21	52.28-30	57
14.28	25	18.13-19.38	30		
15–18	44	18.13	4, 9, 12, 29, 68	*Ezekiel*	
15.1	22, 28, 35-38			1.1-3	50-61
		18.22	48	4	45
15.2	6	18.34-35	48	17–19	60
15.5	22, 44	20	62	17	60
15.6	25	20.20	25	17.3-4	60
15.8	28, 35, 37, 44	21.17	25	17.22-24	60
		21.25	25	18	60
15.11	25	23	15	24.1	15-16
15.13	28	23.21-23	58	33.21	15-16, 55, 57
15.17	6, 18, 28	23.28	25		
15.19-20	67	23.29-30	30, 51	36.20-32	95
15.21	25	24.5	25	38–39	95
15.23	18, 28, 35-36	24.8-17	30	38.4	95

38.11	95	*Daniel*		*2 Chronicles*	
39.23	95	1.1-2	92	13.20	26
40–48	58-59	9.2	92	21.4	40
40.1	58-59	9.24-27	2-3, 76-98,	21.6	39
46.17	59		110-111,	22.2	40
			113	36.10	57-58
Hosea		10–12	92	36.21	90, 92
2.16-17	102	11.2-4	91-92		
		11.2	90		
Joel		11.4	90		
4	95	11.13-14	85		
		11.22	93		
Zechariah					
12–14	96	*1 Chronicles*			
12	95-96	3.17-24	94		
13.7-9	96	5.17	44		
14	95-96	16.1	27		
14.2-4	95				

INDEX OF AUTHORS

Ahituv, S. 73
Albright, W.F. 5-7, 24, 54
Amit, Y. 105
Andersen, K.T. 19
Athas, G. 39
Avigad, N. 72

Bartlett, J.R. 109-10
Begrich, J. 8-9, 15, 19, 22, 26, 40, 46-47, 66
Ben-Shlomo, D. 73
Bergsma, J.S. 59
Bickerman, E.J. 31
Biran, A. 39
Blum, E. 74
Bright, J. 6
Budde, K. 54

Callaway, P.R. 84
Carr, D.M. 72
Cazelles, H. 32
Clines, D.J.A. 14, 77
Collins, J.J. 85, 89, 91-94
Cogan, M. 31
Cook, S.A. 38
Cross, F.M. 84

Davies, P. 84
Demsky, A. 72
Dietrich, W. 71
DiLella, A. 93
Dubberstein, W.H. 16, 30

Emerton, J.A. 56

Finegan, J. 14
Finkelstein, I. 71
Flint, P.W. 92

Galil, G. 3, 12-15, 22, 26, 32, 35, 38, 42, 46, 68, 99
Gooding, D.W. 22
Gray, J. 19

Grayson, A.K. 29-32, 51, 56, 64-66
Green, A.R. 22

Halpern, B. 12, 38, 74, 105
Hanhart, R. 8
Hanson, P. 94
Hartman, L.F. 93
Hayes, J.H. 6, 10-11, 16, 19, 32, 38, 46, 65-66
Herrmann, J. 55
Hoffmeier, J.K. 104
Hooker, P.K. 10-11, 16, 19, 32, 38, 46
Horst, P.W. van der 108-109
Hughes, J. 11-12, 24, 42, 47, 65, 82, 103, 106-108, 110-11

Jacobus, H.R. 107
Jamieson-Drake, D.W. 71
Jepsen, A. 8-9, 15, 38, 40, 42, 46, 66

Kitchen, K.A. 6, 64
Klein, R.W. 107
Klijn, A.F.J. 86-87
Koch, K. 79, 90-92, 96
Kratz, R. 74, 92
Kuhrt, A. 7
Kutsch, E. 16, 32, 52, 54-58

Laato, A. 48, 59, 74, 88, 95, 104
Lacocque, A. 85
Lang, B. 54
Larsson, G. 19, 24, 107
Lemaire, A. 12, 38, 105
Lemche, N.P. 25
Levey, S.H. 55
Lewy, J. 29
Lim, T. 86
Lundberg, M.J. 74

Malamat, A. 2, 16, 52, 56-57, 69, 104
Marti, K. 79, 95
Mazar, E. 73

Index of Authors

McCarter, P.K. 72, 74
McComiskey, T.E. 89
McFall, L. 3
Meyers, C.L. 32
Millard, A. 30, 66, 72-73
Miller, J.M. 6, 65-66
Mitchell, H.G. 95
Montgomery, J.A. 79, 89, 92
Murnane, W.J. 20

Na'aman, N. 20, 22, 44, 47, 63-64, 66, 71, 73
Naveh, J. 39
Neusner, J. 89
Niemann, H.M. 71
Nowack, W. 95

O'Connor, M. 32

Parker, R.A. 16, 30, 64
Pavlovsky, V. 28
Plöger, O. 79
Porteous, N.W. 79, 90, 92
Puech, E. 73

Rabinowitz, I. 83
Reade, J. 44
Redditt, P.L. 94
Reicke, B. 91
Rendsburg, G. 39
Roddy, N. 87
Rollston, C.A. 72-74
Rowley, H.H. 84
Rudolph, W. 95-96

Sanders, S.L. 72, 74
Sass, B. 72
Schiffman, L.H. 86
Schniedwind, W.M. 39, 72
Schürer, E. 78, 90

Segal, M. 110
Shea, W.H. 22
Shedl, C. 23, 32
Shenkel, J.D. 22
Silberman, N.A. 71
Spieckermann, H. 74
Stade, B. 95
Steck, O.H. 44
Stenring, K. 24
Strand, K.A. 7
Strange, J. 38, 40

Tadmor, H. 2, 31, 32, 66-67
Talmon, S. 14
Tappy, R.E. 72, 74
Taylor, S.G. 54-55
Tetley, M.C. 2
Thiele, E.R. 7-8, 15, 17-21, 33, 35, 42, 67
Toorn, K. van der 72
Torrey, C.C. 54

VanderKam, J. 86
Vaux, R. de 80
Vermes, G. 84, 86
Vogt, E. 28, 57

Wacholder, B.Z. 107-108
Waddell, W.G. 107
Weippert, H. 38
Wellhausen, J. 95, 98
Westermann, C. 106
Whitley, C.F. 55
Wiesenberg, E. 83
Williamson, H.G.M. 40
Wiseman, D.J. 30, 51, 56, 69

Yadin, Y. 89

Zimmerli, W. 16, 47, 54
Zuckerman, B. 74

www.ingramcontent.com/pod-product-compliance
Lightning Source LLC
Chambersburg PA
CBHW070945230426
43666CB00011B/2571